MAR 17 2006

OUR
ENDANGERED
VALUES

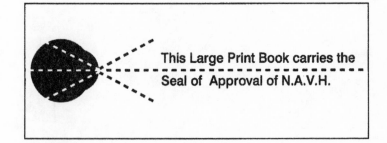

OUR ENDANGERED VALUES

AMERICA'S MORAL CRISIS

JIMMY CARTER

Thorndike Press • Waterville, Maine

Published in 2006 by arrangement with
Simon & Schuster, Inc.

Thorndike Press® Large Print Americana.

The tree indicium is a trademark of Thorndike Press.

The text of this Large Print edition is unabridged.
Other aspects of the book may vary from the original edition.

Set in 16 pt. Plantin.

Printed in the United States on permanent paper.

Library of Congress Cataloging-in-Publication Data

Carter, Jimmy, 1924–
    Our endangered values : America's moral crisis /
by Jimmy Carter.
        p. cm.
    Originally published: New York : Simon & Schuster,
c2005.
    ISBN 0-7862-8309-2 (lg. print : hc : alk. paper)
    1. Social values — United States.   2. Religious
fundamentalism — United States.   3. Christianity and
politics — United States.   4. Church and state — United
States.   5. Church and social problems — United States.
6. Human rights — Government policy — United States.
7. Large type books.   8. United States — Politics and
government — 2001 — Moral and ethical aspects.
9. United States — Foreign relations — 2001 — Moral and
ethical aspects.   10. United States — Moral conditions.
I. Title.
HN90.M6C37 2006
    306.0973′090511—dc22   2005030561

Dedicated to our children
and grandchildren,
for whom America's basic
moral values must be preserved

As the Founder/CEO of NAVH, the only national health agency solely devoted to those who, although not totally blind, have an eye disease which could lead to serious visual impairment, I am pleased to recognize Thorndike Press* as one of the leading publishers in the large print field.

Founded in 1954 in San Francisco to prepare large print textbooks for partially seeing children, NAVH became the pioneer and standard setting agency in the preparation of large type.

Today, those publishers who meet our standards carry the prestigious "Seal of Approval" indicating high quality large print. We are delighted that Thorndike Press is one of the publishers whose titles meet these standards. We are also pleased to recognize the significant contribution Thorndike Press is making in this important and growing field.

Lorraine H. Marchi, L.H.D.
Founder/CEO
NAVH

* Thorndike Press encompasses the following imprints: Thorndike, Wheeler, Walker and Large Print Press.

CONTENTS

Introduction   9

1. America's Common Beliefs —
      and Strong Differences   16
2. My Traditional Christian Faith   26
3. The Rise of Religious
      Fundamentalism   43
4. Growing Conflicts Among
      Religious People   50
5. No Conflict Between Science
      and Religion   64
6. The Entwining of Church
      and State   70
7. Sins of Divorce and
      Homosexuality   84
8. Would Jesus Approve Abortions
      and the Death Penalty?   91
9. Must Women Be Subservient?   110
10. Fundamentalism in
      Government   120

11. The Distortion of American
    Foreign Policy   130
12. Attacking Terrorism, Not
    Human Rights?   147
13. Protecting Our Arsenals, but
    Promoting Proliferation   168
14. Worshiping the Prince of
    Peace, or Preemptive War?   182
15. Where Are the Major Threats
    to the Environment?   203
16. The World's Greatest Challenge
    in the New Millennium   221
17. Conclusion: What Is a
    Superpower?   246

Acknowledgments   250

INTRODUCTION

Americans cherish the greatness of our homeland, but many do not realize how extensive and profound are the transformations that are now taking place in our nation's basic moral values, public discourse, and political philosophy.

Our people have been justifiably proud to see America's power and influence used to preserve peace for ourselves and others, to promote economic and social justice, to raise high the banner of freedom and human rights, to protect the quality of our environment, to alleviate human suffering, to enhance the rule of law, and to cooperate with other peoples to reach these common goals.

With the most diverse and innovative population on earth, we have learned the value of providing our citizens with accurate information, treating dissenting voices and beliefs with respect, and accommodating free and open debate on controversial issues. Most of our political leaders have extolled state and local autonomy, attempted to control deficit spending, avoided foreign adventurism, minimized long-term peace-keeping commitments, preserved the separation of church and state, and protected civil liberties and personal privacy.

All of these historic commitments are now being challenged.

Most of the crucial and controversial issues that we confront were debated long before I became president. These controversies are natural, and most are unavoidable. They involve abortion, the death penalty, science versus religion, women's rights, the separation of religion and politics, homosexuality, America's foreign policy and our global image, civil liberties, the threat of terrorism, nuclear proliferation, the prevalence of guns, the choice between war and peace, environmental quality, and justice for the poor.

More recent debates over these same issues have caused almost unprecedented divisions within our country, with both Democratic and Republican Parties relying on vituperative commercials to win elections, congressional deliberations increasingly characterized by partisan animosity, and our entire population having adopted "red" and "blue" as habitual descriptive phrases within and between states.

What has aroused these sharp disputes and, at the same time, engendered such profound departures from America's traditional values? One factor is our nation's reaction to the terrorist attack of September 11, 2001, as we realized the intensity, permanence, and global nature of terrorism. Another change is that massive sums of money are being injected into the political process, with unprecedented influence of special interests within the increasingly secretive deliberations of government.

The most important factor is that fundamentalists have become increasingly influential in both religion and government, and have managed to change the nuances and subtleties of historic debate into black-and-white rigidities and the personal derogation of those who dare to disagree. At the same time, these religious and political conservatives have melded their efforts, bridging the formerly respected separation of church and state. This has empowered a group of influential "neoconservatives," who have been able to implement their long-frustrated philosophy in both domestic and foreign policy.

The influence of these various trends poses a threat to many of our nation's historic customs and moral commitments, both in government and in houses of worship.

Narrowly defined theological beliefs have been adopted as the rigid agenda of a political party. Powerful lobbyists, both inside and outside government, have distorted an admirable American belief in free enterprise into the right of extremely rich citizens to accumulate and retain more and more wealth and pass all of it on to descendants. Profits from stock trading and income from dividends are being given privileged tax status compared to the wages earned by schoolteachers and firemen. To quote a Christian friend, the new economic philosophy in Washington is that a rising tide raises all yachts.

The irresolvable differences of opinion on abortion, homosexuality, and other sensitive social issues have been exacerbated by the insistence of intensely committed hard-liners on imposing their minority views on a more moderate majority.

Our nation has declared independence from the restraints of international organizations and has disavowed many long-standing global agreements, including judicial decisions, nuclear arms accords, controls on biological weapons, environmental protection, the international system of justice, and the humane treatment of prisoners. Even with our troops involved in combat and America facing the threat of additional terrorist attacks, we have neglected alliances with most of the very nations we need to have join us in the long-term fight against global terrorism. All these political actions have been orchestrated by those who believe that the utilization of our nation's tremendous power and influence should not be constrained by foreigners. Regardless of the costs, some leaders are openly striving to create a dominant American empire throughout the world.

Based on these premises, it is no longer considered necessary to observe restraints on attacking other nations militarily, provided often uncertain intelligence sources claim that their military or political policies might eventually be dangerous to the United States. When branded an "axis of evil," they are pariahs no longer acceptable as negotiating partners, and the lives of their people tend to become relatively inconsequential.

Fortunately, these national policies and this disharmony have not yet become permanent, as many members of the general public, legislators, federal judges, Christians, and other believers are still searching for harmonious answers to most of the controversial religious and political questions. It is in America's best interests to understand one another and to find as much common ground as possible.

After a lifetime of involvement in religious and public affairs, I can understand how sincere are those who have promoted these recent changes. I have experienced the intensity of patriotism as a submarine officer, the ambitions of a competitive businessman, and the intensity of political debate. I have been sorely tempted to launch a military attack on foreigners, and have felt the frustration of having to negotiate with allies or even former enemies to reach a consensus instead of taking more decisive unilateral action.

It has been a struggle for me to withstand pressures from cherished constituents in my political decisions as a state senator, governor, and president. Despite what I consider to be a constitutional and biblical requirement for the separation of church and state, I must acknowledge that my own religious beliefs have been inextricably entwined with the political principles I have adopted.

14

As a private citizen, I will deliberately mix religion and politics in this book. In part of the text I will analyze moral values from a religious point of view, and then include my assessment of the adverse impact of recent political decisions on these same values. I will express my opinions as frankly as possible, as a "born again" evangelical Christian and a former political leader. In the religious realm, I shall depend on the Holy Scriptures, as interpreted by the words and actions of Jesus Christ. On political issues, I shall rely as much as possible on my own personal experiences and observations.

I realize that many readers, even those who share a similar religious and political background, will find some of my opinions to be different from their own. Quite likely, many of them do not realize what is happening in America, and it may be beneficial to raise the issues to the level of increased debate.

1

AMERICA'S COMMON BELIEFS — AND STRONG DIFFERENCES

The most controversial issues being addressed within our nation will be discussed in the following chapters. It will be helpful to understand the prevailing personal opinions of American citizens, their differences and similarities, how they have been modified or remain the same, and whether they are compatible with the profound political changes taking place in our country.

Stronger and sharper partisan differences have evolved among Americans in recent years, quite a departure from when I was in the White House. In those days, I had a good "batting average" in having my proposals accepted by the Congress, and the political divisions were based much more on issues than on whether members were Democrats or Republicans. As a Southern moderate and former career naval officer, I espoused a conservative fiscal policy and a strong defense. A commitment to human rights came, I guess, from my personal knowledge of the devastating effect of racial segregation in my region of the country.

Soon after arriving in Washington, I was surprised and disappointed when no Democratic member of Congress would sponsor my first series of legislative proposals — to reorganize parts of the federal bureaucracy — and I had to get Republicans to take the initiative. Thereafter, my shifting coalitions of support comprised the available members of both parties who agreed with me on specific issues, with my most intense and mounting opposition coming from the liberal wing of the Democratic Party. (One reason for this was the ambition of Senator Ted Kennedy to replace me as president.)

Nowadays, the Washington scene is completely different, with almost every issue decided on a strictly partisan basis. Probing public debate on key legislative decisions is almost a thing of the past. Basic agreements are made between lobbyists and legislative leaders, often within closed party caucuses where rigid discipline is paramount. Even personal courtesies, which had been especially cherished in the

U.S. Senate, are no longer considered to be sacrosanct. This deterioration in harmony, cooperation, and collegiality in the Congress is, at least in part, a result of the rise of fundamentalist tendencies and their religious and political impact.

Fortunately, this degree of rigidity and confrontation has not yet taken hold among the general public. In preparing this book I have searched for the best assessments of American public opinion, so that I could understand the reasons for, and the extent of, agreements and divisions among our people.

A strong majority of both Democrats and Republicans agree that our country is more politically divided than at any time in living memory, a fact that is partially explained by the doubtful presidential election of 2000 and the almost unchanging split during the following years between "red" and "blue" states. Partisan differences of support and disapproval of our two most recent presidents are quite clear, with the personal popularity of President Bush among Democrats lower than was President Clinton's among Republicans while his impeachment proceedings were under way. The ongoing Iraqi war is especially indicative, with diametrically opposite opinions on whether the conflict is going well or has improved national security.

These sharp disagreements might be written off as just partisan wrangling, but their impact on our nation's present and future international policies is significant. Among Republicans, the percentage endorsing diplomacy in preference to military action is minimal, while Democrats take the opposite point of view. In the approach to combating terrorism, two-thirds of Republicans believe that use of overwhelming force is best, while an even larger proportion of Democrats think that, although our armed forces should be used when our nation's security is threatened, excessive use of military action tends to increase animosity against our country and breed more terrorists. This sharp and growing difference over the issue of whether international disputes can be better resolved by diplomacy or by military action is now the *most accurate predictor* of party affiliation — more important than gay marriage, homosexuality, or abortion.

It is encouraging that Americans overwhelmingly agree on several important questions: the value of religion in individual lives, the power of personal initiative to realize human potential, the need to protect the environment even if that is costly, doubt about the integrity of big business, and a desire for federal obscenity laws against hard-core pornography to be enforced vigorously.

Although the number is small, four times as many Republicans as Democrats think that tough environmental laws hurt the economy. There has been a substantial increase in the number of Republicans who have confidence in government, with little difference now between the parties in that regard. Americans also increasingly support more government assistance for the poor and needy, but one remaining difference is that many more Republicans than Democrats believe that poor people have easy lives. It is encouraging that this prejudice against the poor is decreasing significantly among all Americans.

There are strong differences about social issues, but many opinions are changing and most of them have little clear impact in the political arena. The intensity of feeling about controversial issues is often much more important than the numerical divisions. This is especially apparent when the subject of debate is abortion or gun control, where the opinion of a persistent majority of Americans has had little effect in the political world.

A majority of Americans think that abortions should be legal in all or most cases, and only one in six believes that all abortions should be illegal. The fervor and activism of this small minority greatly magnify their influence, especially within the U.S. Congress.

Concerning gun control, an overwhelming majority believe in the right to own weapons, but four of five Americans prefer modest restraints on handguns, including a background check, mandatory registration, and a brief waiting period before one is purchased.

A disturbing change in government policy has involved the firearms industry. Supported by succeeding Presidents Reagan, Bush, and Clinton, legislation was passed by Congress in 1994 that for ten years prohibited the manufacture, transfer, and possession of nineteen specific semi-automatic assault weapons, including AK-47s, AR-15s, and UZIs. None of these are used for hunting — only for killing other humans. More than eleven hundred police chiefs and sheriffs from around the nation called on Congress and President Bush to renew and strengthen the federal assault weapons ban in 2004, but with a wink from the White House, the gun lobby prevailed and the ban expired.

This is not a controversy that involves homeowners, hunters, or outdoorsmen. I have owned and used weapons since I was big enough to carry one, and now own a handgun, four shotguns, and two rifles. I use them carefully, for harvesting game from our woods and fields and during an occasional foray to hunt with my family and friends in other places. We cherish these rights, and some of my companions like to collect rare weapons.

But many of us who participate in outdoor sports are dismayed by some of the more extreme policies of the National Rifle Association (NRA) and by the timidity of public officials who yield to their unreasonable demands. Heavily influenced and supported by the firearms industry, their primary client, the NRA has been able to mislead many gullible people into believing that our weapons are going to be taken away from us, and that homeowners will be deprived of the right to protect ourselves and our families. There are no real threats to our "right to bear arms," as guaranteed by the U.S. Constitution. If so, the NRA efforts would certainly be justified.

In addition to assault weapons, the gun

lobby protects the ability of criminals and gang members to use ammunition that can penetrate protective clothing worn by police officers on duty, and assures that a known or suspected terrorist is not barred from buying or owning a firearm — including an assault weapon. The only criteria that the NRA has reluctantly accepted are proof of a previous felony, mental derangement, or being an illegal immigrant. Deeply concerned when thirty-five out of forty-four men on the terrorist watch list were able to buy guns during a recent five-month period, the director of the FBI began to reexamine the existing law and asked some U.S. senators to consider amendments. The response of top officials in the NRA was to criticize the watch lists — not the terrorists — and to announce support for legislation that protects gun manufacturers and dealers from liability if a buyer uses an AK-47 in a terrorist attack. They also insist that background information on gun buyers be discarded within twenty-four hours, precluding the long-term retention of data that might reveal those who are plotting against our nation's security.

What are the results of this profligate ownership and use of guns designed to kill people? According to the Centers for

Disease Control and Prevention, American children are sixteen times more likely than children in other industrialized nations to be murdered with a gun, eleven times more likely to commit suicide with a gun, and nine times more likely to die from firearms accidents.

The Johns Hopkins Center for Gun Policy and Research reports that the rate of firearm homicide in the United States is nineteen times higher than that of 35 other high-income countries combined. In the most recent year for which data are available, handguns killed 334 people in Australia, 197 in Great Britain, 183 in Sweden, 83 in Japan, 54 in Ireland, 1,034 in Canada, and 30,419 in the United States. The National Rifle Association, the firearms industry, and compliant politicians should reassess their policies concerning safety and accountability.

When asked if they personally believe it is acceptable for gays and lesbians to engage in same-sex behavior, a majority of Americans respond affirmatively, which is a strong shift in opinion since twenty years ago, when responses to the same question were the reverse. There is some indication that this change of public opinion has had an impact among state and federal judges.

The views of Americans have also been changing regarding the death penalty, with support for "life without parole" now at about half and only one-third believing that the death penalty deters crime. In a nationwide poll, only 1 percent of police chiefs thought that expanding the death penalty would reduce crime. This change in public opinion also seems to be having an effect, both in state legislatures and in the federal courts.

These figures paint an overall picture of the beliefs of American citizens, surprisingly unchanged during the past five years. However, revolutionary changes have taken place in our government's domestic and foreign policies, affecting the definition and protection of "moral values."

As an American who has been deeply involved in the political life of our country, I find these statistics to be very interesting. As with almost all other citizens, however, my private life has been the major factor in shaping my own opinions and my personal reactions to the collective views of others.

2

MY TRADITIONAL CHRISTIAN FAITH

To a surprising degree, religious faith has been injected into the political realm in recent years, and a description of my beliefs may be helpful to the reader in assessing my credentials and understanding the reasons for some of my judgments.

I was born into a Christian family, nurtured as a Southern Baptist, and have been involved in weekly Bible lessons all my life, first as a student and then, from early manhood, as a teacher. My basic, or traditional, beliefs were most persuasively presented to me by my father, who was a deacon and my Sunday school teacher at Plains Baptist Church. Although we often had discussions about the meaning of the weekly lesson texts (divided equally between the New Testament and the Hebrew Scriptures), there was no thought of questioning the standard theology that characterized our devotion.

Most of the rudiments of my faith in Christ as Savior and the Son of God are still shared without serious question by Protestants, Roman Catholics, Eastern Orthodox, Copts, Seventh-day Adventists, and many other religious people. We also absorbed some special characteristics of our Baptist denomination. For us, baptism was only for those mature enough to have personal faith in Christ, and by total immersion underwater, symbolizing the death, burial, and resurrection of our Savior. We received the Holy Scripture in its entirety as the revealed will of God, agreeing that the words and actions of Jesus Christ are the criteria by which the Holy Bible is to be interpreted. Although often helpful, human interpretations of the Scriptures were not to be regarded as infallible or as official creeds or instruments of doctrinal accountability.

We believed in the principle of autonomy for each local church, with decisions made by a vote (it is hoped a consensus) of its baptized members. Even within the church congregation, Baptists were adamantly opposed to dominance over individual members by pastors or any other powerful persons, and we emphasized scriptural passages that described how Jesus refrained from giving even his own disciples authority over other people. In his charge to them to go out as witnesses, they were empowered only to serve others, by alleviating suffering and espousing truth, forgiveness, and love. In fact, every person with faith in Christ was considered to be a priest, free to relate directly to God without any intermediary. Local pastors were to be servant ministers and not masters of the congregation.

As evangelicals, we were committed to a strong global mission to share our Christian faith with all other people, without prejudice or discrimination. We fulfilled this mandate of Jesus Christ either by our own personal witnessing or through supporting others with our regular financial offerings. During most of my life it was assumed that our Baptist churches would be members of the Southern Baptist Convention, whose primary purpose was to coordinate our common missionary work in America and around the world. This did not imply, however, that convention officers or any other outside religious leaders could define a set of beliefs or rules that we would have to accept. Our only such description of our faith was the Holy Bible itself.

One of our most fervent commitments

was to the complete separation of church and state. This was an issue of great importance, and we studied Christian martyrs who had sacrificed their lives rather than let any secular leader encroach on religious freedom. Although individual Christians (including my father) were free to take part in public affairs, we abhorred the concept of church congregations becoming involved in the partisan political world. We also believed in religious freedom, compassion for unbelievers, and respect for *all* persons as inherently equal before God.

At least one Sunday each year was devoted to protection of the environment, or stewardship of the earth. My father and the other farmers in the congregation would pay close attention to the pastors' sermons, based on such texts as "The earth is the Lord's, and the fullness thereof." When humans were given dominion over the land, water, fish, animals, and all of nature, the emphasis was on careful management and enhancement, not waste or degradation.

I have used the past tense in the paragraphs above, but these are still my fervent religious beliefs, as an evangelical Christian and a Baptist.

The term "evangelical" is often misused or distorted, but I consider the two primary meanings (*Random House Dictionary of the English Language*) to be quite adequate: (*a*) "belonging to or designating Christian churches that emphasize the teachings and authority of the scriptures, especially of the New Testament, in opposition to the institutional authority of the church itself, and that stress as paramount the tenet that salvation is achieved by personal conversion to faith in the atonement of Christ"; or (*b*) "designating Christians, especially of the late 1970s, eschewing the designation of fundamentalist but holding to a conservative interpretation of the Bible."

Since my mother and my wife were Methodists, I always assumed that equally devout Christians could have different worship and organizational customs and still practice our faith in harmony. It is disturbing to hear prominent Baptists make statements such as "You say you're supposed to be nice to the Episcopalians and the Presbyterians and the Methodists and this, that, and the other thing. Nonsense. I don't have to be nice to the spirit of the Antichrist" (Pat Robertson, *The 700 Club*).

As a midshipman at the U.S. Naval Academy, I taught Bible lessons to the children of officers and enlisted men assigned to serve in Annapolis. It was during this time that I began to explore more deeply the ideas of some prominent theologians. Later, when I was running for governor, I mentioned that I found Reinhold Niebuhr's books to be especially helpful, and I was pleased several months later when his wife, Ursula, sent me a collection of his taped sermons.

My entry into politics both expanded and challenged my religious beliefs. As a state senator, I had about seventy-five thousand constituents for whom I felt responsible, and I was almost overwhelmed with the diversity and importance of the questions and problems they brought to me. In 1966, after serving two terms in the legislature, I set my sights on a campaign for governor. It was an unprecedented and complex political year in Georgia, during which the long-established domination of Democrats was challenged. I did well as a relatively unknown newcomer to state politics, but a quirk in the state constitution permitted the legislature to choose Lester Maddox as the ultimate winner. He had become notorious as a segregationist who threatened with a pickax handle any potential black customers who approached his restaurant in Atlanta for service.

With my defeat, I became thoroughly

disillusioned with politics, and for the first time, my faith was shaken — both in myself and in my religious beliefs. I had never before failed to achieve any of my major goals in life, and I could not understand how God had ordained that a fervent segregationist would be the chief executive of my state. My sister Ruth Carter Stapleton was a famous evangelist in those days, and she understood the egoistic fallacies that caused my despair.

She drove down from North Carolina to see me, and reminded me of scriptural lessons that tragedies and disappointments should be a source of increased patience, strength, wisdom, and commitment to our Christian life. I rejected her premises at first, but Ruth finally convinced me to relegate my political and business ambitions to a secondary position of importance for a while and to assume some challenging religious commitments.

I was soon involved in what Baptists called "pioneer mission" work. My first assignment was in Lock Haven, Pennsylvania, where a hundred families had been identified who had no religious faith of any kind. Another volunteer and I were to visit all these nonbelievers and explain to them the essence of our Christian faith. At first we were overwhelmed with doubt and timidity, but we soon learned to approach each house or apartment on our list with complete faith. We figured out what we could do and say, divided up the responsibilities, prayed a lot, and then tried to relax and depend on God to do the rest. We had some challenging adventures with burly laborers, business executives, avowed atheists, and even the madam of a small whorehouse, but the overall result of our efforts was a series of extraordinary successes.

One of my other, similar missions was to Springfield, Massachusetts, where my assignment was witnessing to Spanish-speaking families, most of whom were from Puerto Rico. They were very poor and lived in old apartment buildings near an abandoned textile mill. Many of them were bused to nearby fields of vegetables and shade-grown tobacco, where they worked as migrant laborers. My partner this time was a Cuban-American named Eloy Cruz, the pastor of a small church in Brooklyn, New York. He said I was chosen to work with him because I had studied Spanish at Annapolis, but we soon realized that the vocabulary I had known and used in the navy was quite different from the one we were now using to teach the gospel!

I was able to read the Bible verses that we chose for each visit, but Reverend Cruz did almost all the witnessing. I was amazed at how effectively he could reach people's hearts. They would become quite emotional and sometimes weep when he explained to them some aspect of Jesus' ministry and how His life could relate to them. I had wonderful experiences every day as I worked with this remarkable man, who seemed to form an almost instant intimacy with the poor people whose homes we entered. I was as overwhelmed as they, and several times had tears running down my cheeks.

I was embarrassed by the deference with which Reverend Cruz treated me, possibly because I was a native-born American, owned an automobile, and had been a state senator. As we prepared to say good-bye at the end of our mission, I asked him what made him so gentle but effective as a Christian witness, and he was quite disconcerted. He finally said, *"Pues, nuestro Señor no puede hacer mucho con un hombre que es duro"* (Well, our Lord cannot do much with a man who is hard). He noted that Christ himself, although the Son of God, was always gentle with those who were poor or weak. He went on to say that he tried to follow a simple rule: "You only need two loves in your life: for God, and for the person in front of you at any particular time."

I still refer on occasion to the books on my shelves by Karl Barth, Reinhold and H. Richard Niebuhr, Paul Tillich, Rudolf Bultmann, Dietrich Bonhoeffer, Hans Küng, and other theologians, but Eloy Cruz's simple words express a profound and challenging theology that has meant more to me than those of all the great scholars.

I did evangelical work in other communities, and had an especially interesting experience as the manager of a Billy Graham crusade in my own county. Since the evangelist couldn't be with us, we used one of his films to present the religious message. This was still a time of racial segregation, but I followed Graham's rule of requiring integrated planning sessions and audiences. Since no church would accept us, we were forced to have committee meetings in an abandoned school building and to present the film in the local movie theater. The results were amazing, with several hundred people, without racial distinctions, coming forward to accept Jesus Christ as Savior.

After I was elected governor, my family became members of Northside Drive Baptist Church, the nearest one to the governor's mansion in Atlanta, and I served as a deacon and assumed other normal duties. We followed the same pattern when we moved to Washington, joining the congregation of First Baptist Church, where I also taught a few times each year. These sessions were never publicized in advance, so that our regular Sunday school class members were usually the only ones in attendance.

It was intriguing to observe the interest of self-described atheists in my Christian faith. In my first year as president I visited Poland, where I wished to speak publicly about the value of freedom among the nations that were under Soviet domination. During my conversation with the country's leader, Communist First Secretary Edward Gierek, I mentioned a previous visit with the Roman Catholic prelate of Poland, Stefan Cardinal Wyszynski. Gierek asked that I join him for a private session, and we talked for quite some time about my Christian faith. Gierek's mother, a devout Catholic, had been to the Vatican and had seen the pope, and the first secretary seemed to be torn between her faith and being a loyal Communist. I felt that privately he was a Christian, but publicly an atheist.

Later, while visiting South Korea, I had somewhat heated discussions with President Park Chung Hee about his human rights violations, American troop deployments, and other subjects of international importance. As I was preparing to leave the president's office after my last official visit, he asked if he could discuss a private matter, and we excused the other members of our entourages. He described the religious faith of two of his children, one a Buddhist and the other a Christian, and asked me to explain the rudiments of my faith to him. I did so, and we concluded our discussion with an agreement that I would arrange for one of South Korea's most noted Baptists to pursue the subject further. A few months later, Park was assassinated by the head of South Korea's intelligence service, who succeeded him as president. I never knew the final outcome of our religious discussion.

One of my most interesting and perhaps most productive conversations was with the Chinese leader Deng Xiaoping, with whom I negotiated normal diplomatic relations between the United States and the People's Republic of China. During his state visit to Washington, Deng and I had a number of wide-ranging talks about many aspects of

Chinese and American life, in order to establish as firm a friendship as possible between our two peoples. At a state banquet one evening, he asked what inspired my first interest in his country. I replied that I was raised as a Baptist and that our pre-eminent heroes were the women Christian leaders who went to China as missionaries to spread the gospel about Jesus Christ. Even as a little child, I gave five cents a month to help build schools and hospitals for Chinese boys and girls.

Deng was amused by my response, and pointed out that religious activities of that kind had been terminated when the People's Republic of China was established in 1949. Under the Communist regime, in fact, the official government policy was atheism, and worship services and the distribution of Bibles and other holy books were prohibited. I asked if it might be possible to change these policies, and he asked for specific suggestions. After a few moments' thought, I made three requests: guarantee freedom of worship, permit the distribution of Bibles, and reopen the door to missionaries. Before returning to China, Deng Xiaoping told me that the basic law of China would be changed to provide for religious freedom and that Bibles would be authorized. However, he would not approve the return of Western missionaries because, he said, they had "lived like royalty" and had tried to subvert the lifestyles of the Chinese people. Within three years, he had kept both his promises, with a proviso that any new church congregations would register with the government. They could then conduct services freely, as desired.

I have described these three encounters with political leaders to illustrate the interest, even of nonbelievers, in Christianity. They were all private discussions, and I tried to honor that confidentiality during the lifetimes of these foreign officials. This was the standard premise with which Rosalynn and I treated other aspects of our religious life while I held public office.

A few years ago a religious magazine tried to encapsulate such premises, and I was asked to express my definition of success in life — in just fifty words! I was in a quandary about how to respond, until I remembered an experience I had in 1974, while I was governor. I was invited by Dr. Norman Vincent Peale to go with him to Macon, Georgia, to join in presenting an award from his *Guideposts* magazine to the nation's outstanding church congregation of the year. He said there would be about seven thousand people assembled in the municipal center to honor the Church of the Exceptional, a congregation of about fifty mentally retarded people.

I knew about Dr. Peale's great ability as an inspirational speaker, and I felt somewhat competitive as I prepared my own address. He and I gave our best speeches, and then came the final event: the lighting of a large candle by one of the church members. She was a middle-aged woman with Down syndrome, who came slowly but proudly down the center aisle carrying a lighted taper. She was followed closely by the pastor of the little church, who offered to steady her and give her assistance. She rejected all help, and approached the candle with obvious confidence and pride.

The small flame wavered back and forth, and despite her repeated efforts, the candle wouldn't light. The crowd sat with bated breath, and Dr. Peale and I couldn't avoid a feeling of embarrassment for her. The pastor moved forward and put his hand on hers to steady the taper, but she shook her head and pushed him away.

Finally, the candle lit, and the crowd erupted into applause. But the brightest thing in the huge auditorium was the woman's face, which glowed with happiness.

It is quite unlikely that anyone there that night, more than thirty years ago, would remember anything that Dr. Peale or I had to say in our carefully prepared speeches. But no one will ever forget the triumphant moment when the woman demonstrated her own dedication, confidence, achievement, and pride in having contributed to the evening ceremony honoring her little church. Seven thousand lives were touched by her faith and determination.

It was primarily from this experience that I chose fifty words in answer to the magazine's inquiry:

I believe that anyone can be successful in life, regardless of natural talent or the environment within which we live. This is not based on measuring success by human competitiveness for wealth, possessions, influence, and fame, but adhering to God's standards of truth, justice, humility, service, compassion, forgiveness, and love.

Since leaving the White House, I have been a professor at Emory University for almost a quarter century, and have lectured often in the theology school and the religion department, where I found my rudimentary acquaintance with theology to be helpful in answering students' questions. Also, Rosalynn and I make a special effort to be home in Plains on Sundays, and I teach a Bible class between thirty-five and forty times each year at Maranatha Baptist Church to our own adult members and to the visitors who come. These sessions are filmed and tape-recorded and distributed widely. I can't say whether my theological studies have been very helpful in these hometown classes, where I never deviate in any appreciable way from expressing the traditional Christian beliefs that I inherited from my father.

Of the several hundred visitors who attend my Sunday lessons each week, only about 15 percent happen to be Baptists. When I take a few minutes to let my class identify themselves, there are usually about a half dozen "mainline" Protestant denominations represented, often accompanied by Roman Catholics, Amish, Mennonites, Mormons, Quakers, and Seventh-day Adventists. Our church welcomes Jews, Muslims, and other non-Christian worshipers, and we encourage everyone to take part in the discussions. They are quite interesting and helpful to me, and over the years I have acquired an insight into the beliefs and interests of many other religious people.

3

THE RISE OF
RELIGIOUS FUNDAMENTALISM

In my 2002 Nobel speech in Oslo, I said, "The present era is a challenging and disturbing time for those whose lives are shaped by religious faith based on kindness towards each other." When asked by *Christianity Today* to explain this statement, I responded:

"There is a remarkable trend toward fundamentalism in all religions — including the different denominations of Christianity as well as Hinduism, Judaism, and Islam. Increasingly, true believers are inclined to begin a process of deciding: 'Since I am aligned with God, I am superior and my beliefs should prevail, and anyone who disagrees with me is inherently wrong,' and the next step is 'inherently inferior.' The ultimate step is 'subhuman,' and then their lives are not significant.

"That tendency has created, throughout the world, intense religious conflicts. Those Christians who resist the inclination toward fundamentalism and who truly follow the nature, actions, and words of Jesus Christ should encompass people who are different from us with our care, generosity, forgiveness, compassion, and unselfish love.

"It is not easy to do this. It is a natural human inclination to encapsulate ourselves in a superior fashion with people who are just like us — and to assume that we are fulfilling the mandate of our lives if we just confine our love to our own family or to people who are similar and compatible. Breaking through this barrier and reaching out to others is what personifies a Christian and what emulates the perfect example that Christ set for us."

There has been, indeed, a disturbing trend toward fundamentalism in recent years, among political leaders and within major religious groups both abroad and in our country, and they have become increasingly intertwined. I felt the impact of this movement for the first time when

Ayatollah Khomeini assumed the leadership of Iran, branded the United States of America "the Great Satan," and encouraged his young and militant followers to hold fifty-two of our embassy personnel captive for fourteen months. This shameful action was a direct violation of international law; and his fundamentalist interpretations of the Islamic Holy Scriptures, on which he based his religious leadership, also contravened the traditional teachings of the Koran concerning peace, compassion, and specifically the benevolent treatment of visitors or diplomats from other nations.

A few weeks before our hostages were seized in Iran, the newly elected president of the Southern Baptist Convention came to the Oval Office to visit me. This had been a routine ceremony for many years, especially when the president of the United States happened to be a Baptist. I congratulated him on his new position, and we spent a few minutes exchanging courtesies. As he and his wife were leaving, he said, "We are praying, Mr. President, that you will abandon secular humanism as your religion." This was a shock to me. I considered myself to be a loyal and traditional Baptist, and had no idea what he meant.

Later, after attending worship services at First Baptist Church, I met with our pastor and asked him to explain the troubling comment. He replied that a small group of conservative Southern Baptist leaders had marshaled adequate political support at the convention to elect the new president, an event about which I had been only casually aware. Without knowing how further to answer my questions, he surmised that I had made some presidential decisions that might be at odds with political positions espoused by leaders of the newly formed Moral Majority and other groups of conservative Christians. Some of the things we considered were that I had appointed many women to high positions in government, rejected using government funds in religious education, established an independent Department of Education to enhance the public schools, accepted the *Roe v. Wade* abortion decision of the Supreme Court, worked with Mormons to resolve some of their problems in foreign countries, normalized diplomatic relations with the Communist government of China, called for a Palestinian homeland and refused to move the U.S. embassy from Tel Aviv to Jerusalem, and was negotiating with the Soviet Union on nuclear arms control and other issues.

Both my pastor and I were still in a quandary, but I had no alternative except to ignore the condemnation and continue doing what I thought was best for our country (and also compatible with my traditional Baptist beliefs). At the same time, I began to learn what I could about both Islam and the generic aspects of fundamentalism.

For generations, leaders within my own church and denomination had described themselves as "fundamentalists," claiming that they were clinging to the fundamental elements of our Baptist beliefs and re-sisting the pressures and influence of the modern world. This inclination to "cling to unchanging principles" is an understandable and benign aspect of religion, and a general attitude that I have shared during most of my life.

I soon learned that there was a more in-tense form of fundamentalism, with some prevailing characteristics:

- Almost invariably, fundamentalist movements are led by authoritarian males who consider themselves to be superior to others and, within religious groups, have an overwhelming commitment to subjugate women and to dominate their fellow believers.

- Although fundamentalists usually believe that the past is better than the present, they retain certain self-beneficial aspects of both their historic religious beliefs and of the modern world.

- Fundamentalists draw clear distinctions between themselves, as true believers, and others, convinced that they are right and that anyone who contradicts them is ignorant and possibly evil.

- Fundamentalists are militant in fighting against any challenge to their beliefs. They are often angry and sometimes resort to verbal or even physical abuse against those who interfere with the implementation of their agenda.

- Fundamentalists tend to make their self-definition increasingly narrow and restricted, to isolate themselves, to demagogue emotional issues, and to view change, cooperation, negotiation, and other efforts to resolve differences as signs of weakness.

To summarize, there are three words that characterize this brand of fundamentalism: rigidity, domination, and exclusion.

4

GROWING CONFLICTS AMONG RELIGIOUS PEOPLE

The very existence of the early Christian church was endangered by divisive arguments, such as whether one had to become a circumcised Jew and follow the laws of the Torah before accepting Christ as Savior, whether it was permissible to eat meat that had been offered to pagan gods, which day of the week was to be considered holy, and which of the apostles would be the preeminent interpreter of the ministry of Jesus Christ. The healing factor was a realization that drawing nearer to Christ reduced the importance of human differences and brought people closer to one another.

It has been estimated that there were only a thousand Christians in 40 A.D., seven years after the death and resurrection of Jesus Christ. As the local congregations gained strength and influence, the scattered believers came under terrible persecution from other religious leaders and from Roman conquerors. Because of successful efforts to resolve their own theological differences and, later, the powerful Christian influence of Emperor Constantine, within three centuries the number of professed Christians had increased to approximately 30 million, or about 55 percent of the citizens of the vast Roman Empire.

There are now about 2 billion Christians, or one-third of the world's population, but it is likely that modern-day believers in Christ are more sharply divided than Christians in those earliest days. It is inevitable during any historical era for Christians to disagree on some social and religious issues, and perfectly legitimate, even admirable, for us Americans to promote our personal beliefs through either religious or political processes. It is interesting that our many different denominations are relatively aloof from one another and rarely competitive, with no significant debates between Baptists, Methodists, and Episcopalians or even between Protestants and Catholics. But deep within each Protestant denomination and also among Roman Catholics there are various disagreements that have torn believers apart, one from another, and have sometimes even split denominations permanently and officially.

As an evangelical Christian, I am deeply concerned about the many divisive arguments that have driven these deep wedges between us. The most highly publicized differences involve social issues, but many of our disputes have religious connotations that arouse little interest among non-Christians, such as the priesthood of believers, the autonomy of local churches, the servant-hood of pastors, the role of women in churches, Calvinism, dispensational premillennialism, inerrancy, creationism, and more secular issues like academic freedom in our colleges and seminaries.

Even among fellow church members with whom Rosalynn and I have worshiped, there are wonderfully devout believers who accept every word in the Bible (preferably the King James Version) as literally true. Their faith in our Creator entails the belief that the universe was created during six rotations of the earth on its axis and that the first woman emerged from Adam's rib about six thousand years ago, both she and he originally conceived in their present human form. We accept the sincerity of their faith without question. Even though some people are obsessed with these issues, it is fruitless and counterproductive to argue about matters of this kind.

We Christians can buttress our arguments on almost any subject by careful selection of certain Scripture verses, and then claim that they should be applied universally. Almost invariably, the divisions among Christians are based on the presumption of preeminence by one group over others. It is very difficult to honor the many admonitions of Saint Paul, and Jesus' own words: "Judge not, that ye be not judged." Deviation from his admonition can lead to ignoring, condemning, or even persecuting those who are different or considered to be inferior in some way. Many of us Baptists were distressed when the elected president of our convention declared that God does not hear the prayers of a Jew.

Beginning about twenty-five years ago, some Christian leaders began to form a union with the more conservative wing of the Republican Party. Such a political marriage is in conflict with my own belief in the separation of church and state — I would feel the same even if the marriage were with Democrats.

Now, leaders of the highly organized Christian Right have successfully elevated into America's political debate some of the most divisive social questions. The most vivid examples involve sexual preference, which obviously has highly personal and emotional overtones. Tragically, these divisive social questions have even been moved to the forefront of the presidential election scene. At the same time, almost all Protestants now condone divorce as acceptable, and rarely emphasize fornication or adultery, although these sexual acts were repeatedly condemned by Jesus. It is much easier and more convenient to focus on sins of which we are not known to be guilty.

Protestant church congregations, and especially Baptists, have always been inclined to divide because of theological issues, social questions, or personal disputes, and this may be one reason for our enormous expansion. Our own Maranatha Baptist Church in Plains was formed while I was in the White House by a small group who were more moderate on some issues than our parent church, including the acceptance of black worshipers and welcoming other visitors. But more recently throughout Christendom, the admixture of social and theological issues has brought increasingly intense acrimony, and this pattern seems also to prevail among Jews and Muslims.

After we left the White House, Rosalynn and I began to observe changes within the political and religious arenas of American life, and their slow but steady confluence. We had no idea how profound the impact of this revolution would be, both on us personally and on our nation.

We became active in our hometown church, which had always been affiliated with the Southern Baptist Convention, and were relatively casual observers of the conservative coalition steadily gaining more leadership positions and then coming to dominate convention affairs. Their next steps were to begin imposing their theological decisions on others, and dramatically to reduce the level of academic freedom. Although I deplored some of the new policies of our convention and the growing alignment of its leaders with the Republican Party, my continuing hope was to see the healing of differences among Baptists so that we could work together in our global evangelical efforts.

After the divisions became deeper and other efforts failed, I decided to invite a wide range of influential Baptists to my office at The Carter Center, in Atlanta, to explore chances for some degree of reconciliation. Surprisingly, the positive response was almost unanimous, and we had thirty moderate and conservative leaders join me. Everyone agreed that no critical comments would be made about one another or any persons who were not present. When I proposed that a joint statement of mutual respect and common purpose might be helpful, they asked me to submit a draft to them. After some editing, twenty-six of the participants signed, including six men who had been or would be presidents of the Southern Baptist Convention, and the text was widely publicized.

The statement acknowledged that there were divisive issues among us that we wished to resolve through prayer, and we promised to treat one another as brothers and sisters in Christ. We also pledged to promote religious freedom and to form alliances with Christians of other cultures and ethnic groups.

This provided a pleasant but all-too-brief interlude, as the verbal debates continued and the convention adopted increasingly restrictive policies. A major and perhaps permanent schism occurred at the annual Southern Baptist Convention in 2000, when a new "Baptist Faith and Message" statement was adopted. Of preeminent concern to many Baptists was the deletion of the previously stated premise that "the sole authority for faith and practice among Baptists is Jesus Christ, whose will is revealed in the Holy Scriptures." In effect, this change meant substitution of Southern Baptist leaders for Jesus as the interpreters of biblical Scripture. Although there were solemn pledges that acceptance of this new statement would be voluntary, it soon became obvious that it would be imposed as a mandatory creed on all convention officers, employees, deans and professors of colleges and seminaries, and even missionaries who were serving in foreign countries. The strictness of this mandatory compliance has exceeded that in the Roman Catholic Church or within other Protestant denominations.

The new creed was troubling enough, but it was combined with other departures from historic Baptist beliefs, including the melding of religion and politics, domination by all-male pastors, the exclusion of traditional Baptists from convention affairs, the subservience of women, encroachments on the autonomy of local churches, and other elements of the new fundamentalism. It became increasingly obvious that our convention leaders were really in conflict with traditional or mainstream Christians. After much prayer and soul-searching, Rosalynn and I decided to sever our personal relationships with the Southern Baptist Convention, while retaining our time-honored Baptist customs and beliefs within our own local church.

Almost total dominance of Baptist pastors over laypersons has been implemented, based on this statement of a prominent conservative leader, W. A. Criswell: "Lay leadership of the church is unbiblical when it weakens the pastor's authority as ruler of the church." This premise violates Jesus' announcement that he was a servant, that his disciples would be servants, and that the greatest would be servant of all. There was certainly no biblical use of the word "ruler," but this self-promotion of pastors was made official in 1988, and now applies generally throughout the Southern Baptist Convention, most state conventions, and especially the megachurches.

The most recent move is the convention leaders' decision to withdraw from the Baptist World Alliance, an international organization that the Southern Baptist Convention helped to organize and in which it played a key role for a century. Their surprising claim is that the BWA has suddenly become too "liberal" for their continued association — a claim deeply resented by heroic European Christians who fought the oppression of Soviet Communism and endangered their lives by clinging to their traditional religious heritage.

This focus on events within my own religious denomination may not be especially interesting to some readers, but it has had a profound impact on every American citizen through similar and related changes being wrought in our nation's political system. During the last quarter century, there has been a parallel right-wing movement within American politics, often directly tied to the attributes of like-minded Christian groups. The revolutionary new political principles involve special favors for the powerful at the expense of others, abandonment of social justice, denigration of those who differ, failure to protect the environment, attempts to exclude those who refuse to conform, a tendency toward unilateral diplomatic action and away from international agreements, an excessive inclination toward conflict, and reliance on fear as a means of persuasion.

When I teach my Bible classes, I try to explain the essence of our faith and inspire listeners to correlate Christianity with their own daily lives. The divisive debates that seem to obsess the modern Christian community do not match very closely the messages I usually choose. One Sunday I asked a large class, mostly visitors, to name the items now being discussed most widely among their various denominations. In addition to some social issues, they quickly named mandatory prayer in schools, use of public funds to support religious education, the service of women as leaders, evolution, public display of the Ten Commandments, the autonomy of local congregations, forced acceptance of creeds, the exaltation of pastors, and the breakdown of barriers between church and state.

There was no mention of theological or religious questions that involved our common goal of worldwide evangelism, or how to implement the teachings of Jesus Christ in our daily lives. It was clear that much of our energy is spent in internecine warfare, in arguments and debates that not only are divisive but tend to incapacitate us as we work in the name of Christ. We agreed that there was still a gratifying degree of harmony within most local congregations, and that the arguments were at a higher organizational level.

When there is an expression of favoritism, domination, or animosity within the religious community, it tends to authenticate the same attitudes among secular or even governmental groups who have personal prejudices. It is no accident that our Christian churches, at least in the South, have been well known as the last bastions of racial segregation. Also invidious, and now quite openly and generally accepted, is discrimination against women. These kinds of religious decisions are based on highly selective choices of Scripture by dominant white males, and ignore the overall premise of the actions and teachings of Jesus and leaders of the early Christian church.

The many differences among Christians create confusion, fragmentation, and even acrimony, and it is difficult for individual believers to comprehend and adhere to the fundamental elements of our faith. The broader consequence of all these divisions is that global evangelical work suffers and our reputations are tarnished as we contend with one another. Instead, religion should provide the way to heal the differences that separate people, based on the paramount law that Jesus taught, to love our neighbors as ourselves.

Perhaps the most broad and inclusive

range of opinion among American Protestants is within the National Association of Evangelicals, a group with which I feel compatible on most issues. In addition to the protection of life, their agenda places a heavy emphasis on peace, the restraint of violence, strengthening of family life, protection of children, justice and compassion for the poor and vulnerable, the preservation of religious liberty, the safeguarding of human rights, and protection of the environment. In their latest statement, in April 2005, there is a call for strict "just war" restraints on the initiation of armed conflict, with war only as a last resort, plus an expression of concern about global warming. Not surprisingly, leaders of the religious right opposed the majority of evangelicals on these latter two issues.

There are notable precedents for Christians to absorb strong differences and still work together to further God's kingdom. The early church survived when the fundamentals of faith offered adequate bonds to overcome dissension and unite the fallible and argumentative Christians. Perhaps, once again, we might be reconciled through emulating the actions and teachings of Christ and following the entreaty of Saint Paul to the early churches:

"Now I beseech you, brethren, in the name of our Lord Jesus Christ, that ye all seek the same thing, and that there be no divisions among you; but that ye be perfectly joined together in the same mind and in the same judgment."

To the Church in Corinth

"Now the God of patience and consolation grant you to be like-minded one toward another according to Christ Jesus: that ye may with one mind and one mouth glorify God, even the father of our Lord Jesus Christ."

To the Church in Rome

5

NO CONFLICT
BETWEEN SCIENCE
AND RELIGION

One of the most ancient and persistent debates, especially in the United States, has been between science and religion. I was chairman of the Sumter County Board of Education during the early 1960s, and the famous Scopes "monkey" trial in Tennessee was still a subject of frequent discussion, even after thirty-five years had passed. We were aware of debates among school administrators both in Georgia and in other states about teaching evolution, but we managed to avoid contention on this issue in our county — perhaps because dealing with racial integration of the public school system provided enough controversy to keep everyone occupied.

I am thankful that this dichotomy between the two opposing forces has never been either a political or a personal problem for me. As a graduate student and as one of the earliest participants in utilizing nuclear power for peaceful purpose, I was eager to expand my knowledge of physics and the other sciences. This did not, in any way, threaten my religious faith, since I had been fortified since childhood with the frequently recited Bible verse "Now faith is the substance of things hoped for, the evidence of things not seen" (Hebrews 11:1).

I had always understood that we didn't need scientific proof of the existence or character of God. In fact, whenever there was adequate physical evidence to prove any theory or proposition, then we didn't need faith as a basis for our belief. Even for those without specific religious convictions, the inner feeling of what was right and wrong and the awe-inspiring beauty of starlit sky or sunset, the emergence of a butterfly from a chrysalis, the industry of an ant, or the sprouting of a seed were adequate proofs of God's hand in our lives and in creation.

It seems obvious to me that, in its totality, the Bible presented God's spiritual message, but that the ancient authors of the Holy Scriptures were not experts on geology, biology, or cosmology, and were not blessed with the use of electron microscopes, carbon-dating techniques, or the Hubble telescope. I've never been bothered by verses in the Bible stating that the earth is flat or has four corners, that stars can fall on the earth like figs from a tree, or that the world was created in six calendar days as we know them.

Whenever there is a scientific discovery or a theory that is proven by the observation of facts, these are just additional revelations to fallible human beings of truths that have always existed. They cannot possibly have an adverse effect on the status of the omnipotent Creator of the entire universe. As scientists discover or reveal new information about the natural world, the discoveries must be correlated with one another in innovative theories. Each theory is then intensely and rigidly tested by subsequent observations, which provide either additional proof and acceptance or error and rejection. This is how truth is revealed.

The existence of millions of distant galaxies, the evolution of species, and the big bang theory cannot be rejected because they are not described in the Bible, and neither does confidence in them cast doubt on the Creator of it all. God gave us this exciting opportunity for study and exploration, never expecting the Bible to encompass a description of the entire physical world or for scientific discoveries to be necessary as the foundation for our Christian faith.

One of my favorite writers on scientific subjects was Stephen Jay Gould, with whom I corresponded on occasion. In 1989 he wrote what I consider the most enjoyable of his books, *Wonderful Life: The Burgess Shale and the Nature of History.* Although some of his theses were later disputed by other paleontologists, I thoroughly enjoyed the descriptions of the weird creatures that had emerged from a transforming climatic change about 500 million years ago. He referred to their subsequent evolution as something like a tape going through a machine, with the results being attributable to a completely haphazard recording.

I wrote him a private letter, expressing my belief that there had obviously been some logic or order in the process. He didn't respond directly, but subsequently quoted and slyly ridiculed my opinion in one of his monthly magazine articles, later part of a book. About two years before he died in 2002, he sent me a copy of *Rocks of Ages*, his intriguing book that was designed to resolve the conflict between science and religion. His approach was to separate the two completely, in what he called "nonoverlapping magisteria." The great observations of science would define the natural world, and the overall teaching (magisterium) of religion would define the spiritual world, and they should not intrude on each other.

For me, this was an acceptable approach. There is no place for religion in the science classroom, but it will not end the committment of some devout Christians to reject all aspects of Charles Darwin's explanation of evolution or any geological discoveries that indicate an earth that is more than six thousand years old. Neither did Gould's approach match my own personal belief that God created the universe and that new scientific discoveries, when proven, must be accepted even if they are not compatible with some of the biblical descriptions of creation and the centrality and configuration of the earth and heavens.

There will always be people who insist on one aspect of knowledge to the exclusion of the other and are plagued with the realization that religion and science cannot prove each other. This doesn't bother me. We are all born with free will, to accept or reject whatever we choose. At the same time, we have no right to deprive other people of the freedom to study and to accept or reject propositions that are put forward as truths.

Many years ago, I wrote a poem that expresses my own difficulty in comprehending it all:

A Contemplation of What Has Been Created, and Why

I tried to fathom nature's laws
From twirling models and schoolroom
*   sketches*
Of molecules and parts of atoms,
And nearly believed — but then came
*   quarks,*
Bosons, leptons, antiparticles,
Opposite turning mirror images,
Some that perforate the earth,
Never swerving from their certain paths.
I've listened to conflicting views
About the grand and lesser worlds:
A big bang where it all began;
Of curved, ever-expanding space;
Perhaps tremendous whirling yo-yos
That will someday reach the end
Of cosmic gravity and then
Fly back to where they can restart
Or cataclysmically blow apart —
And then, and then the next event.
And is it all an accident?

I feel sure that it is not all an accident.

6

THE ENTWINING
OF CHURCH AND STATE

During the last two decades, Christian fundamentalists have increasingly and openly challenged and rejected Jesus' admonition to "render to Caesar the things that are Caesar's and to God the things that are God's." Most Americans have considered it proper for private citizens to influence public policy, but not for a religious group to attempt to control the processes of a democratic government or for public officials to interfere in religious affairs or use laws or tax revenues to favor certain religious institutions.

Although the issue was prominent when John Kennedy's Catholicism was debated, I also reintroduced, inadvertently, the subject of religious faith into a presidential campaign. One April night in 1976 at the home of a North Carolina political supporter I was asked point-blank if I was a "born again Christian." There were news reporters there, and I truthfully answered, "Yes," assuming that all devout Christians were born again, of the Holy Spirit. This was the first time that this religious character-ization had been injected into the political arena, and there was an immediate furor, with media allegations that I claimed to be receiving messages directly from heaven and thought that I was endowed by God with some elements of sanctity and superi-ority over other candidates. From then until the end of the campaign, national reporters made a big deal of what had seemed natural to me and my Baptist hosts, making clear to me that injecting religion into politics was a mistake.

Rosalynn and I had a wonderful oppor-tunity to violate this basic principle when I had a cautious inquiry in 1979 from the Vatican about a possible visit from Pope John Paul II, less than a year after he was elected to the papacy. I was delighted to send an official invitation, and this became the first (and only) papal trip to Washington, D.C. The new pontiff was already demon-strating his commitment to call on as many of his parishioners as possible, and had been to a number of Latin American nations. He made a leisurely visit, spending almost two days in the capital area, and we had time for some long discussions.

His Holiness had a wonderful sense of humor and, in addition to several other languages, spoke English well. We recalled how much animosity there had been when John Kennedy ran for president, with allegations that if he was elected, the American people would see the pope in the White House. When I introduced John Paul to some visiting congressmen, I pointed out that the predictions of the Protestant protesters — nineteen years earlier — had finally come true!

I expressed my gratitude for the pope's efforts to reach out to other Christians and also to Jews and Muslims, and for his obvious commitment to instill a global vitality in the church. He seemed to welcome a free exchange of views, and I disagreed with him on his perpetuation of the subservience of women and their exclusion from the priesthood, which I considered to be a departure from their roles in the early Christian church. This was a harmonious exchange, but there was more harshness when we turned to the subject of "liberation theology," which is still a matter of sharp debate in Latin America.

Most countries in the area were ruled by

military dictators at that time, and many priests and bishops, whom I considered to be heroes, were speaking out sharply in protecting the rights of oppressed poor and indigenous people. Invariably, John Paul II condemned the human rights activists and supported the more orthodox church leaders, who were aligned with despotic and abusive regimes. I thought he was more interested in loyalty to the Vatican than to those who endangered their own lives and priestly status by ministering to the people who were suffering. The extremely conservative organization Opus Dei (Work of God) was given strong support from the Vatican (its founder was later canonized a saint), and its leaders had great influence in the church. In the pope's defense, my national security adviser, Zbigniew Brzezinski, pointed out that John Paul was heavily influenced by his background in Poland and his knowledge of other Eastern European countries, where the priests or bishops who disagreed with Rome were inclined to be Communists. Nevertheless, this and other Vatican policies have resulted in a massive shift of Catholics to Protestant congregations.

I enjoyed a visit to the Vatican on a subsequent trip to Italy, and Rosalynn and our daughter, Amy, later paid their personal respects to the pontiff. Although I felt closer to the theology and pronouncements of Pope John XXIII, there is no doubt that John Paul II was a truly great leader, with deep moral convictions and an unequaled ability to express his Christian beliefs to the world. There has never been a more charismatic and popular pope.

I was careful to separate my official status as president from the private worship habits of my family, but I worked behind the scenes with Southern Baptist Convention president Jimmy Allen to develop what we called "Bold Mission Thrust," an innovative convention program designed to expand the global evangelistic effort of Baptists. I prayed more during those four years in the White House than at any other time in my life, primarily for patience, courage, and the wisdom to make good decisions. I also prayed for peace — for ourselves and others, especially Israel and its neighbors. When Iran was holding our hostages, I asked for their safe return to freedom.

Since the publication of my religious books, *Living Faith* and *Sources of Strength*, I have been asked whether my Christian beliefs ever conflicted with my secular duties as president. There were a few inconsistencies, but I always honored my oath to "preserve, protect, and defend the Constitution of the United States." For instance, I have never believed that Jesus Christ would approve either abortions or the death penalty, but I obeyed such Supreme Court decisions to the best of my ability, at the same time attempting to minimize what I considered to be their adverse impact.

Jesus proclaimed that his ministry was to "bring good news to the poor, to proclaim freedom for the prisoners, recovery of sight for the blind, and to release the oppressed." This statement has always been well known to Christians, but after a lifetime of responsibilities in both religious and political arenas, I reached what was, to me, a surprising and somewhat reluctant conclusion. In efforts to reach out to the poor, alleviate suffering, provide homes for the homeless, eliminate the stigma of poverty or racial discrimination, preserve peace, and rehabilitate prisoners, government officeholders and not church members were more likely to assume responsibility and be able to fulfill the benevolent missions.

The government and the church are two different realms of service, and those in political office have to face a subtle but important difference between the implementation of the high ideals of religious faith and public duty. In a speech to my fellow Baptists in 1978, I tried to explain the duality of my personal responsibilities as a president and as a Christian:

"Thomas Jefferson, in the original days of our country, said he was fearful that the church might influence the state to take away human liberty. Roger Williams, who created the first Baptist church in our country, was afraid that the church might be corrupted by the state. These concerns led to the First Amendment, which prohibits the establishment of any official state church and, in the same sentence, prohibits the passing of any laws that might interfere with religious freedom.

"Separation is specified in the law, but for a religious person, there is nothing wrong with bringing these two together because you can't divorce religious beliefs from public service. At the same time, of course, in public office you cannot impose your own religious beliefs on others.

"In my office in the White House I have to deal with many domestic and international problems: peace, freedom, nuclear explosives, the sale of weapons, terrorism, rapidly expanding populations without adequate food or health care. But this is more than a list of political problems. These are also moral problems for you and me, because they involve the very precepts of God in which we believe.

"I want our country to be strong enough in all elements, military and otherwise, so we never have to prove we are strong.

"Reinhold Niebuhr, in his book *Moral Man and Immoral Society*, pointed out the difference between a society and people. The expectations from a person are a much higher standard. A person should have as our goal complete *agape*, self-sacrificial love. The most we can expect from a society is to institute simple justice.

"So, we as people have to do better, particularly if we are blessed with the opportunity to demonstrate our worth. Leaders also have to be careful not to be too timid.

". . . A country will have authority and influence because of moral factors, not its military strength; because it can be humble and not blatant and arrogant; because our people and our country want to serve others and not dominate others. And a nation without morality will soon lose its influence around the world.

"What are the goals of a person or a denomination or a country? They are all remarkably the same: a desire for peace; a need for humility, for examining one's faults and turning away from them; a commitment to human rights in the broadest sense of the words, based on a moral society concerned with the alleviation of suffering because of deprivation or hatred or hunger or physical affliction; and a willingness, even an eagerness, to share one's ideals, one's faith with others, to translate love in a person to justice."

During the twenty-seven years since I made that speech, there has been a much more public effort to break down what Thomas Jefferson espoused as "a wall of separation between church and state."

Referring to this premise, *700 Club* host Pat Robertson said, "There is no such thing in the Constitution. It's a lie of the left, and we're not going to take it anymore."

He repeatedly attacks public schools and calls for their replacement with religious academies.

Chief Justice William Rehnquist, in a U.S. Supreme Court minority opinion, has written, "The 'wall of separation between church and state' is a metaphor based on bad history, a metaphor which has proved useless as a guide to judging. It should be frankly and explicitly abandoned."

In 2000, Southern Baptist Convention leaders dropped from their new creed "The state has no right to impose taxes for the support of any form of religion." They have subsequently espoused vouchers for private schools and a constitutional amendment to authorize mandatory prayer in public schools, and they are openly challenging "the strict separation of church and state."

Government funding of social programs through "faith-based initiatives" appeals to religious groups who have no qualms about breaking down the historic wall between religion and government. They substitute certain charitable services in a religious environment for more broad and equitable government programs that address the wider needs of the poor for economic justice, with access to training for jobs, affordable housing, health care, sound education, and a livable wage. These initiatives bypass the historic implementation of the First Amendment by channeling taxpayers' dollars to churches and other religion-based providers of social services under contrived rules that allow for proselytizing and putting religious tests on hiring employees. The initiative even provides taxpayers' money to build and renovate houses of worship. There is no doubt that the goal is to finance programs that are clearly religious, and the annual level of somewhat surreptitious government funding through religious institutions has now reached about $2 billion.

Perhaps one of the strangest and most disturbing examples of this political effort by right-wing Christians has been to attack the federal court system itself, after Senate Democrats failed to approve a handful of the most conservative nominees for federal judgeships. They ignored the fact that this was the same number as Republicans had successfully opposed among Bill Clinton's nominees. Senator Bill Frist, the highest-ranking member of the United States Senate, aligned himself in a public telecast with a fundamentalist religious group to promote false claims that Democratic senators who opposed a few judges were conducting "an assault against people of faith." The group's leader announced that the "activist" judiciary poses "a greater threat to representative government" than "terrorist groups." Dr. James Dobson, another sponsor of the event, called the Supreme Court "unaccountable," "out of control," and "a despotic oligarchy," and accused the justices of a forty-year "campaign to limit religious liberty." (At a subsequent press conference, President George W. Bush disavowed the connection between religious faith and opposition to the appointment of federal judges.)

In fact, most of the judges who are targets of this well-orchestrated religious attack are devout Christians. Ten of the thirteen federal appeals courts actually have a majority of Republican appointees, as does the U.S. Supreme Court, which elected a president in 2000 with a five-to-four partisan ruling. In effect, Senator Frist was helping to promote the premise that any senators who vote against extremely conservative judicial nominees are opposed to a right-wing brand of state religion. This may be a violation of the U.S. Constitution, at least in spirit, which prohibits any government effort to impose religious views on Americans.

Shortly after announcing her retirement in July 2005, Supreme Court Justice Sandra Day O'Connor declared, "In all the years of my life, I don't think I've ever seen relations as strained as they are now between the judiciary and some members of Congress . . . and it makes me very sad to see it." She continued: "The present climate is such that I worry about the future of the federal judiciary."

Some prominent Republicans have also become deeply concerned about the extraordinary influence of religious groups in their political party. John Danforth, who was an Episcopal priest before representing Missouri in the U.S. Senate, published an editorial in the *New York Times* (April 2005) that said:

"Republicans have transformed our party into the political arm of Conservative Christians. The elements of this transformation . . . are parts of a larger package, an agenda of positions common to Conservative Christians and the dominant wing of the Republican Party. . . . The problem is not with people or churches that are politically active. It is with a party that has gone so far in adopting a sectarian agenda

that it has become the political extension of a religious movement. . . . As a
Senator, I worried every day about the
size of the federal deficit. I did not
spend a single minute worrying about
the effect of gays on the institution of
marriage. Today it seems to be the
other way around."

There is obviously a widespread, carefully
planned, and unapologetic crusade under
way from both sides to merge fundamentalist Christians with the right wing of the
Republican Party. Although considered to
be desirable by some Americans, this
melding of church and state is of deep
concern to those who have always relished
their separation as one of our moral values.

7

SINS OF DIVORCE
AND HOMOSEXUALITY

Sometimes all of us Christians forget the scriptural assertions "All have sinned and come short of the glory of God" and "Judge not, that ye be not judged." It now seems like a humorous incident, but I almost lost the presidential election by attempting to explain these kinds of biblical texts. I'll never forget my own consternation at the reaction when, during the 1976 presidential campaign, I answered a *Playboy* magazine reporter's question about whether I considered myself superior to other Americans because I was a Christian. I quoted some phrases from Jesus' Sermon on the Mount in which he declined to distinguish between those who murdered and had hatred in their hearts, or between adulterers and those who looked on a woman lustfully. I denied having committed adultery, but stated that I had felt sexual desire for some girls I had known. There was a firestorm of criticism from my political opponents and famous church leaders because of my "lust," and within a week I lost 10 percentage points in public opinion polls.

As noted earlier, an interesting characteristic of fundamentalists is an obsession with one or two emotional issues, as with homosexuality among some religious factions. Many devout worshipers respect homosexuals but refuse to give such sexual relationships their religious blessing, while some other groups have chosen gays and lesbians as the foremost targets of their denigration. Leaders of the Southern Baptist Convention, for instance, have elevated homosexuality to a pinnacle of great importance among deviations from their increasingly narrow and rigid definition of the Christian faith.

An even more disquieting claim is that HIV/AIDS is God's punishment on those who have sinned and should be treated accordingly. Jesus had encounters with lepers, who were also looked upon as sinful, condemned by God, and capable of contaminating their neighbors. He set an example for us by reaching out to them, loving, healing, and forgiving them. The public condemnation and ridicule of gays has been increasingly promoted by a few demagogic religious leaders, and the political acceptance of this treatment tends to authenticate and encourage this discrimination.

I remember that immediately after the terrorist attack of 9/11 on the World Trade Towers, Jerry Falwell said, "I really believe that the pagans, the abortionists, the feminists, and the gays and lesbians who are actively trying to make that an alternative lifestyle. . . . I point the finger in their face and say 'you helped this happen.'" Pat Robertson, his host on the *700 Club* television program, quickly agreed.

Other, more moderate Christians and denominations are also struggling with the gay issue, but rarely with the same personal condemnation and exclusion from Christian blessing. The altercations are usually limited to the church's ordination of gay ministers and the performance of religious weddings between gay couples.

Although Jesus Christ never included homosexuality among his very strict reminders of deviations from a perfect life, Saint Paul does include homosexual acts among a long list of his other concerns. But he was always careful to interweave admonitions against the condemnation of others, and as all Christians know, Paul emphasized repeatedly that all of us are sinners, that the wages of sin is death, but that through faith in Christ we can be totally forgiven.

One of my Christian heroes is Dr. Jimmy Allen, the last moderate president of the Southern Baptist Convention. His family has suffered severely from the ravages of AIDS and the refusal of Baptist congregations to accept some suffering members of the Allen family into Christian fellowship. He says, "Our problem is not the definition of sin; it is the understanding of grace . . . if we truly love the person, we can deal with his or her deviant behavior. . . ." He added, "What we have a difficult time doing is to hate the sin, but love the sinner. Admittedly, such a biblically balanced position will not be universally applauded by the gay community. Nor will it be universally accepted by the 'straight' community. But we will hear 'Well done, good and faithful servant' from the one who counts, as we learn to love in the spirit of Christ."

I don't see any prospect for the multiple Christian denominations to resolve completely the debates about the religious status of gays and lesbians, but there is no reason for this issue to drive a wedge between us or for our country to be divided in the political arena. In fact, there is very little difference of opinion on this subject among political parties, with both presidential candidates in 2004 opposing gay marriages but approving legally recognized unions that would provide equal civil rights to gay or lesbian couples. Despite this agreement, the nonissue was hotly debated during the presidential campaign, pushed to the fore-front by a few shrewd political demagogues who promoted defining marriage with an amendment to the U.S. Constitution. They knew this proposal to be politically infeasible, but it kept the issue near the forefront of emotional debate about moral values.

Since the punishment for adultery in the Christian era and more ancient times was death, and since Christ himself strongly condemned both adultery and divorce, a constitutional amendment with more biblical authenticity might be "Adultery and divorce are condemned, and marriage is defined as a legal and spiritual union between a man and a woman until they are parted by death." With a clear majority of Americans condoning divorce and believing it is acceptable for gays and lesbians to engage in same-sex behavior, it may be best to leave the U.S. Constitution alone.

All of us consider family values and the stability of marriage to be extremely important. I never knew a divorced person before I went to college, but divorce has now become alarmingly prevalent. Among all American adults, 25 percent have experienced at least one divorce, with the incidence varying by religious affiliation and age. Among major Christian groups, Baptists are at the top — 29 percent — with Catholics and Lutherans at 21 percent. Except for Asians (only 9 percent), Protestant senior pastors were the lowest group (15 percent). Baby boomers have already reached 34 percent, those between fifty-three and seventy-two years of age 37 percent, and older citizens only 18 percent. There are many reasons for this threat to the sanctity of matrimonial vows, but few would regard homosexuality as a significant factor in this multitude of failed marriages.

Rather than letting the controversial issue remain so divisive among our citizens, perhaps we should separate the two basic approaches, by letting governments define and protect equal rights for citizens, including those of "civil unions," and letting church congregations define "holy matrimony."

A law passed in Connecticut in April 2005, almost by consensus, extends to gay couples the same legal rights guaranteed to married heterosexuals, including family leave, tax and insurance benefits, and hospital visits, with a provision that defines marriage as a union between a man and a woman. This is a logical and simple division of responsibilities between church and state with which I feel comfortable. Our only alternative is to perpetuate the unnecessary religious conflict and wait for the U.S. Supreme Court to give the ultimate answer to the legal questions.

8

WOULD JESUS APPROVE ABORTIONS AND THE DEATH PENALTY?

ABORTION

Of all the sharply debated moral and political issues in America, abortion is the most divisive. Emotions run deep on both sides of the question, and they permeate both our nation's domestic and foreign policy. At the same time, there is a general consensus within our Christian churches that a developing fetus is a human life and should be protected.

It is practically impossible to meld the two most extreme views on abortion, with one side claiming that this is strictly a decision to be made by a woman about her own body with little or no regard for the fetus, and the other maintaining that a human being exists at the instant of conception and that murder results from any interruption of the embryo's development — or even the female ovum's fertilization by ejaculated sperm. There will never be any reconciliation between these true believers.

I am convinced that every abortion is an unplanned tragedy, brought about by a combination of human errors, and this has been one of the most difficult moral and political issues I have had to face. As president, I accepted my obligation to enforce the *Roe v. Wade* Supreme Court ruling, and at the same time attempted in every way possible to minimize the number of abortions — through legal restrictions, prevention of unwanted pregnancies, the encouragement of expectant women to give birth, and the promotion of foster parenthood.

I was bombarded with questions about abortion from the news media throughout my political campaigns and my presidency. One of my best-remembered and most often quoted remarks came at a presidential press conference in July 1977, when I defended my lack of support for federal funds to be used for abortions among poor mothers, even though wealthier women could afford to have their pregnancies terminated. Without any careful forethought, I responded to a question on this issue by saying, "Life is often unfair."

I could see then, and now, a clear opportunity to make substantial reductions in the need or desire for abortions while protecting the basic rights of a pregnant woman as prescribed by the Supreme Court. I advocated the evolution of more attractive adoption procedures, hoping to encourage the birth of a baby who might be unwanted or unplanned, and at the same time meet the desire of would-be parents to obtain a child. My administration also gave top priority to health care for new mothers and their babies.

In summary, I tried to do everything possible to prevent unwanted pregnancies and to encourage prospective mothers to deliver their babies. Without any apologies, I addressed the issue with the somewhat simple approach that "every baby conceived should be a wanted child." Frank and effective sex education is critical for teenagers, with a primary emphasis on abstinence but also information about safe and proven birth control methods.

Many fervent pro-life activists do not extend their concern to the baby who is born, and are the least likely to support benevolent programs that they consider "socialistic." They ignore the fact that once a doubtful mother decides *not* to have an abortion, she and her family usually have a number of needs: continued education for the mother, or a maternity leave from her job; special health care, with insurance to cover the costs; housing allowances; an adequate minimum wage; and tax credits to help the employed mother and her child have a decent life. Two-thirds of women who have abortions claim their primary reason is that they cannot afford a child.

There are two main sources of data on abortions in the United States: the Alan Guttmacher Institute and the Centers for Disease Control, and their latest report (2002) indicates that 47 percent of women who have unintended pregnancies resort to abortion. Six in ten of these women are already mothers, with 40 percent being white, 32 percent black, and 20 percent Hispanic. More than half are in their twenties, and about 15 percent are teenagers. There is no clear pattern of race, age, marital status, or previous children. The most prevailing common factor is poverty, with six out of ten abortions occurring among those with incomes below $28,000 per year for a family of three.

With economic prosperity and strong social services, American abortion rates reached a twenty-four-year low during the 1990s, to a rate of only sixteen per thousand women of childbearing age. It has long been known that there are fewer abortions in nations where prospective mothers have access to contraceptives, the assurance that they and their babies will have good health care, and at least enough income to meet their basic needs.

The most notable examples are Belgium and the Netherlands, where only seven abortions occur among each thousand women of childbearing age. In some predominantly Roman Catholic countries where all abortions are illegal and few social services are available, such as Peru, Brazil, Chile, and Colombia, the abortion rate is fifty per thousand. According to the World Health Organization, this is the highest ratio of unsafe abortions.

One of the well-meaning but counter-productive approaches is to refrain from teaching our young people how to avoid pregnancy, instruction that is provided thoroughly and persistently in other nations. There is now skyrocketing federal funding for sex education, but unfortunately most often with a strict prohibition against mention of any kind of contraception, despite the fact that 60 percent of our American teenagers report having sex before they are eighteen years old. A *New York Times* article reveals that Canadian and European young people are about equally active sexually, but, deprived of proper sex education, American girls are five times as likely to have a baby as French girls, seven times as likely to have an abortion, and seventy times as likely to have gonorrhea as girls in the Netherlands. Also, the incidence of HIV/AIDS among American teenagers is five times that of the same age group in Germany. It is obvious that our teenagers are mature enough to be given the facts about sex, and deserve to be able to protect themselves — preferably by abstinence, but with the wise use of contraceptives if that is their deliberate choice.

Some of our government's international policies are equally counterproductive. In March 2002, Rosalynn and I joined Bill Gates Sr. and his wife, Mimi, in a trip around the periphery of Africa, designed to explore the optimum investment of funds from the Bill & Melinda Gates Foundation in reducing the terrible impact of HIV/AIDS. We met with a wide range of citizens, from prostitutes to national leaders, and we learned that there were notable successes in Uganda and Senegal and terrible failures in Botswana, Central African Republic, and South Africa. Kenya, Ethiopia, and Nigeria seemed to be holding their own, with about 6 percent of the population being HIV-positive.

The most effective approach was a bold presentation of explicit sex education and the use of condoms to prevent the infection, combined with inexpensive retroviral treatment of pregnant women to reduce the incidence of HIV infection among their newborn babies. Although costly, treatment was also needed for already infected adults to ease suffering and prolong life.

There are members of the U.S. Congress who attempt to prevent the use of foreign aid funds for any form of family-planning services in other countries. Now with support from the White House, their amendments are almost invariably inserted into the most benevolent legislation. The impact of this policy is counterproductive if the purpose of the development assistance is to ease pain and suffering, to improve the lives of adults, and to reduce the infant mortality rate.

In private, some of these legislators are quite cynical about Third World countries, while admitting that they are succumbing to rigid pro-life political pressures. They claim that, in any case, the saving of children's lives only contributes to over-population and more future suffering. Surprisingly, statistics reveal just the opposite: parents breed fewer children when their infants have a better chance to survive, with the result that population growth and infant mortality rates are proportionally related, increasing or decreasing together.

The sanctity of life is a basic moral issue, and should be a religious and political commitment. At the same time, there is a balancing act that must be evolved. One hotly debated issue involves stem cell research. It has been proven scientifically that a fertilized human egg (about the size of the period at the end of this sentence) can provide cells that are very flexible in their use, with prospects of preventing or curing a number of diseases, including diabetes, Alzheimer's, Parkinson's, and spinal cord injuries.

With strong public support from distinguished Republicans, including Nancy Reagan and Governor Arnold Schwarzenegger, California voters approved a referendum in 2004 to establish a massive program of stem cell research, and subsequent public opinion polls show that at least three quarters of Americans support such efforts. Despite this public support, some right-to-life activists and President Bush strongly oppose any introduction of new stem cell lines. The president points out that a few older lines are already authorized and states that the question is "whether or not we use taxpayers' monies to destroy life in order to hopefully find cures for terrible disease." The few human stem cell lines available for government-funded research are usable but were grown with mouse cells, a requirement that scientists are working to eliminate. In the meantime, an almost uncontrollable impetus continues for expanded research.

A bipartisan majority of members of the U.S. House and Senate support carefully restricted legislation that would not create any new cells for research but would allow the use of some of the excess frozen embryos in fertility clinics, if parents agree to offer them for this limited purpose. About 2 percent of the estimated four hundred thousand frozen and unused embryos wind up being given to other families who desire children, while the others are being destroyed. The proposed law would permit the use of a few of these, while prohibiting the use of taxpayer money to create new embryos by cloning or other means. Despite these restraints, the president has promised to veto any such legislation.

A startling announcement in May 2005 revealed that South Korean scientists had developed a revolutionary scientific procedure that holds great medical promise. Using cells donated by people suffering from diabetes, spinal cord injuries, and other afflictions, they have created new stem cell lines that can genetically match those of the injured or sick patients.

It is clear that the subject of life before birth will continue to be one of the most hotly debated, in religious, political, and scientific terms. There is a strong religious commitment to the sanctity of human life, but, paradoxically, some of the most fervent protectors of microscopic stem cells are the most ardent proponents of the death penalty.

THE DEATH PENALTY

When I was governor of Georgia, there was an intense competition among my peers in other states to determine which of us could achieve the greatest reduction in our prison populations. We spent a lot of effort on institutional reform, bringing in experts on various means of classifying new inmates to prepare them for basic education, career training, and psychological rehabilitation in prison, all followed by early-release and work-release programs. I was personally involved in the recruitment of volunteers from Lions, Rotary, Civitan, and Kiwanis service clubs who were trained to serve as probation officers, with a singular duty: each had to agree to "adopt" one prospective parolee, become acquainted with the inmate's family back home, and find a job for the person when parole was granted. At that time, in the 1970s, only one in a thousand Americans was in prison.

That policy has been completely abandoned and reversed, as our nation's almost total focus is now on punishment, not rehabilitation. This is a characteristic of fundamentalism: "I am right and worthy, but you are wrong and condemned." More than seven Americans out of a thousand are now imprisoned — most of them for nonviolent crimes. This is the highest incarceration rate in the world, exceeding Russia's former record of six per thousand. Among the busiest construction industries in many states is building more jail cells, and job opportunities for prison guards have skyrocketed. One of my successors as governor of Georgia bragged to my wife that his greatest accomplishment while in office was "building enough prison cells to reach from the state Capitol all the way to my hometown" — a distance of about forty-five miles. Our state's "Two strikes and you're out" law will help to keep this punitive industry flourishing.

In addition to imprisonment, the United States of America stands almost alone in the world in our fascination with the death penalty, and our few remaining companions are regimes with a lack of respect for basic human rights. Ninety percent of all known executions are carried out in just four countries: China, Iran, Saudi Arabia, and the United States. In fact, our nation and Somalia (which has no organized government) are the only two that have refused to ratify the International Covenant on the Rights of the Child, which prohibits execution for crimes committed by children. Since 1990, only seven countries other than the United States had executed people for crimes they committed as juveniles, and even those — Iran, Pakistan, Saudi Arabia, Yemen, Nigeria, China, and the Democratic Republic of the Congo — now have disavowed the practice. Finally, in March 2005 the U.S. Supreme Court voted five-to-four to outlaw juvenile executions

— a decision strongly condemned by many conservative Christians. It seems somewhat illogical to say, "You have violated God's commandment 'Thou shalt not kill,' so therefore I will kill you." Unfortunately, that is the philosophy of a dwindling number but still a slight majority of Americans.

In 1972 the Supreme Court ruled that capital punishment, as it was then administered, was "cruel and unusual" and therefore unconstitutional. On July 1, 1976, however, the court overturned the ruling by a seven-to-two decision, while imposing some restraints, and capital punishment was reinstated. I've always considered myself fortunate that while I was governor and president, there were no executions under my jurisdiction.

One of the key reasons proponents of the death penalty put forward is that it is a strong deterrent to murder and other capital crimes. In fact, the evidence shows just the opposite. The homicide rate is at least five times greater in the United States than in any European country, none of which authorizes the death penalty. The Southern states carry out over 80 percent of the executions but have a higher murder rate than any other region. Texas has by far the most executions, but its homicide rate is twice that of Wisconsin, the first state to abolish the death penalty. It is not a matter of geography or ethnicity, as is indicated by similar and adjacent states: the number of capital crimes is higher, respectively, in South Dakota, Connecticut, and Virginia (all with the death sentence) than in the adjacent states of North Dakota, Massachusetts, and West Virginia (without the death penalty). Furthermore, there has never been any evidence that adding the death penalty reduced capital crimes, or that the crimes increased when executions were prohibited.

Some devout Christians are among the most fervent advocates of the death penalty, contradicting Jesus Christ and justifying their belief on an erroneous interpretation of Hebrew Scriptures. "An eye for an eye, and a tooth for a tooth," their most likely response, overlooks the fact that this was promulgated by Moses as a limitation — a prohibition against taking both eyes or all of an offender's teeth in retribution. Also, we might remember Jesus' explanation that Moses gave these and some other aspects of the Torah, including divorce, to accommodate "the hardness of heart" of his listeners.

The Bible has numerous examples of

mercy as an alternative to the prescribed death sentence, as when God permitted the first known murderer, Cain, to live, and threatened a sevenfold vengeance against anyone who harmed him. Another interesting Scripture is found in Ezekiel 33, where God says, "I have no pleasure in the death of the wicked, but that the wicked turn back from his ways and live." Perhaps the most vivid example of God's forgiveness and restitution is King David, who committed adultery with the beautiful Bathsheba and then had her husband, Uriah, killed. In another dramatic instance, Jesus forgave a woman sentenced to be stoned to death for adultery.

It seems logical that all Christians would follow the example of Jesus Christ, but there is an inexplicable difference between most Protestants and Catholics. The Catholic Church has taken a firm stand against the death penalty, acknowledging that sovereign governments have the legal right to take the life of a guilty person as punishment, but *only* if there is no alternative. Pope John Paul II wrote: "The nature and extent of the punishment must be carefully evaluated and decided upon, and ought not go to the extreme of executing the offender except in cases of absolute necessity

— in other words, when it would not be possible otherwise to defend society. Today, however, as a result of steady improvements in the organization of the penal system, such cases are very rare if not practically nonexistent."

In 1999 in St. Louis, the pope described capital punishment as "cruel and unnecessary," and the same year, on Good Friday, America's Catholic bishops issued this appeal:

"Increasing reliance on the death penalty diminishes all of us and is a sign of growing disrespect for human life. We cannot overcome crime by simply executing criminals, nor can we restore the lives of the innocent by ending the lives of those convicted of their murders. The death penalty offers the tragic illusion that we can defend life by taking life. Through education, through advocacy, and through prayer and contemplation on the life of Jesus, we must commit ourselves to a persistent and principled witness against the death penalty, against a culture of death, and for the gospel of life."

Perhaps the strongest argument against

the death penalty is the extreme inequity in its employment: it is biased against the poor, the demented, and minorities, and designed or at least applied to protect white victims. It is not surprising that since the death penalty was reinstated in 1976, 76 percent of those sentenced to death, even in the federal courts, have been members of minority groups. As a typical example, of the 99 murderers who were executed in 1999, for 127 homicides, 104 of the victims were white! It is almost inconceivable to imagine a rich white person going to the death chamber after being defended in court by expensive trial lawyers, especially if the victim was black or Hispanic.

Recently, with the advent of DNA testing, it has been found that many people on death row are actually not guilty. Illinois governor George Ryan declared a moratorium on executions when he learned that thirteen condemned inmates were innocent of capital crimes, and five of them were subsequently freed completely because of DNA tests. Since 1973, almost 120 inmates in American prisons who had been sentenced to death have been released from death row.

My last book, *Sharing Good Times*, is dedicated "to Mary Prince, whom we love and cherish." Mary is a wonderful black woman who, as a teenager visiting a small town, was falsely accused of murder and defended by an assigned lawyer whom she first met on the day of the trial, when he advised her to plead guilty, promising a light sentence. She got life imprisonment instead, and as a trusty was permitted to serve as a maid in the governor's mansion. She was so outstanding that I asked to be designated as her parole officer, and Mary lived with us for four years in the White House. A reexamination of the evidence and trial proceedings by the original trial judge revealed that Mary was completely innocent, and she was granted a pardon. She was fortunate, and could just as easily have been executed. If the victim had been white, we would never have known Mary Prince.

She would likely have shared the fate of Lena Baker, a black woman who was held in servitude against her will and abused by her master, a white man. On one day in 1945, she was tried, convicted by an all-white jury, and sentenced to death, after confessing that she shot him when he attacked her with a metal bar and threatened to kill her. After a thorough reexamination of the case, she was given a full pardon in

August 2005 — sixty years after dying in the electric chair.

Standing alone among great democratic nations in imposing the death penalty is another moral decision that Americans are being forced to confront. Although the death penalty was supported by a strong majority in the past, public opinion is changing. A recent poll has shown that when informed that DNA tests and other evidence have resulted in the release of many inmates on death row, about two-thirds of Americans support a moratorium on executions.

Another question for Christians: If faced with this choice, what would Jesus do?

9

MUST WOMEN BE SUBSERVIENT?

The Fifteenth Amendment to the U.S. Constitution granted black men the right to vote in 1870, ninety-four years after the declaration "All men are created equal." It was fifty years later that American women finally won the same right, and some slow progress has been realized since that time — at least in the secular world. President Franklin D. Roosevelt selected the first woman to occupy a cabinet post, and other presidents and I have chosen women for major roles in our cabinets and White House staff. I was able to appoint more female federal judges than all my predecessors combined, and a growing number of women are serving as governors, in the House and Senate, and as chief executive officers of major corporations. Other nations as diverse as India, Pakistan, Indonesia, Israel, Great Britain, the Philippines, and

Nicaragua have had women as presidents or prime ministers. These nations represent citizens who are predominantly Hindu, Muslim, Jewish, and Christian, and include two of the three largest democracies on earth.

Despite the fact that Jesus Christ was the greatest liberator of women, some male leaders of the Christian faith have continued the unwarranted practice of sexual discrimination, derogating women and depriving them of their equal rights to serve God. This same insistence on the submission of wives to husbands and the branding of women as inferior has also been adopted in some Islamic nations. It is inevitable that this sustained religious subjugation has been a major influence in depriving women of basic rights within the worldwide secular community.

Most Bible scholars acknowledge that the Holy Scriptures were written when male dominance prevailed in every aspect of life. When Jesus began his remarkable ministry, the treatment of women throughout the Roman Empire and the Holy Land was reminiscent of what we have observed recently under the Taliban regime in Afghanistan. Even in matters of marriage and divorce, women were considered to be chattel, who were not to contradict decisions made by their fathers or husbands. Even widows of prominent and respected men had few legal rights. Men could possess multiple women (King Solomon had three hundred wives and seven hundred concubines), but adulterous behavior by a woman could be punished by stoning to death.

There are two reports in Genesis of God's creation of human beings, which may seem to be somewhat contradictory. It was the sixth day when, as described in Genesis 1:26–27, "God said, 'Let us make humankind in our image, according to our likeness'; . . . so God created humankind in his image, in the image of God he created them; male and female he created them." Then, in the second chapter of Genesis, God first created man and later decided that he needed a partner. "So the Lord God caused a deep sleep to fall upon the man, and he slept; then he took one of his ribs and closed up its place with flesh. And the rib that the Lord God had taken from the man he made into a woman and brought her to the man. . . . Therefore a man leaves his father and his mother and clings to his wife, and they become one flesh."

Both of these Scriptures emphasize mutuality and equality of the worth of male and female, but many Christian fundamentalists use the second selection as a basis for their belief in the superiority of first-created man, combined with an allegation that Eve should be held solely accountable for "original sin." There is no need to argue about such matters, because it is human nature to be both selective and subjective in deriving the most convenient meaning by careful choices from the 30,400 or so biblical verses.

There is one incontrovertible fact concerning the relationship between Jesus Christ and women: he treated them as equal to men. This dramatically differed from the prevailing custom of the times. Although the four Gospels were written by men, they never report any instance of Jesus condoning sexual discrimination or the implied subservience of women. In a radical departure from earlier genealogies, Matthew even includes four gentile women among the ancestors of Christ: Tamar, Rahab, Ruth, and Bathsheba. The exaltation and later worship of Mary, Jesus' mother, is an even more vivid indication of the special status of women in Christian theology.

There are too many examples from the earthly ministry of Christ to describe here, but two or three are pertinent. Despite the prevailing prohibition against any dealing with women in public, Jesus had no hesitancy about conversing at the community well with a Samaritan woman, who was a pariah among both Jews and her peers because of her ethnicity and lascivious behavior. She accepted Jesus as the promised Messiah, and took this message back to her own villagers — the first example of an evangelical witness. Jesus also rejected the double standard of punishment for adultery, by granting both a pardon and forgiveness to a condemned woman, saying simply, "Let him who is without sin throw the first stone."

Perhaps more significant was the adoption of women to travel with Jesus' entourage, and the acceptance of their spiritual and financial support within his personal ministry. It may be that his most intimate confidante was Mary, the sister of Lazarus, whom he visited often in Bethany and who seemed to be one of the few people who understood that he would be crucified and resurrected. Mary Magdalene had the honor of boldly visiting his empty tomb, and then the Savior instructed her to in-form all the other disciples, fearfully hiding in a secret place, that the Savior was risen from the grave.

It is ironic that women are now welcomed into all major professions and other positions of leadership but are deprived of the right to serve Jesus Christ in positions of leadership as they did during his earthly ministry and in the early Christian churches. This is just another contentious issue that has caused divisions within our faith. In fact, a decision to increase prejudicial attitudes based on gender is one of the primary reasons I decided to sever my ties with a denomination to which I had been loyal during the first seventy years of my life.

The current special effort of Southern Baptist Convention leaders to "keep women in their place" is based on the ridiculous assertion that "man was first in creation, and woman was first in the Edenic fall," plus a few careful selections from Saint Paul's letters to the early churches. It does seem clear that, if addressed alone, some verses from Paul's letters to the early churches indicate his departure from Jesus' example and a strong bias against women, directing that they should be treated as second-class

Christians — submissive to their husbands, attired and coiffed demurely, and silent in church.

I do not maintain in any case that the troubling verses are erroneous or that there are contradictions between different portions of the original inspired word of God. It is necessary in some cases, though, to assess the local circumstances within a troubled early church congregation and to study the exact meaning of the Greek and Hebrew words. One illustrative example: Paul says, "I permit no woman to teach or to have authority over a man." The Greek word for "teach or have authority" is *authentein,* and this is the only time it is used in the New Testament. I don't know Greek, but scholars point out that other early meanings of the word included "killing," "originating," "dominating," and "authoring."

Many scholars interpret Paul's instructions to the church in Corinth as descriptive of special problems within some of the congregations, an expression of concern to "brothers and sisters" who are confused and disorderly. For worshipers in our modern society, it has been found convenient to ignore Paul's comments pertinent to his era — such as "Any woman who prays or prophesies with her head unveiled disgraces her head — it is one and the same thing as having her head shaved. For if a woman will not veil herself, then she should cut off her hair." (This makes it clear, by the way, that it is acceptable for women to pray and prophesy if their heads are covered.) Paul also forbade women to braid their hair or to wear rings, jewelry, or expensive clothes. It is obvious to most modern-day Christians that Paul is not mandating permanent or generic theological policies.

In a letter to Timothy, Paul expresses a prohibition against women's teaching men, but we know — and he knew — that Timothy himself had been instructed by his mother and grandmother. It is also difficult to understand how Paul's close friend Priscilla is revered for having instructed Apollos, one of the great preachers of that day, so that he could more accurately reveal that Jesus was indeed the Christ.

To resolve the apparent disharmony between Jesus and Paul in defining the status of women, I refer to two other excerpts from Paul's writings. In his letter to the Galatians, Paul states, "But now that faith has come, we are no longer subject to a disciplinarian, for in Christ Jesus you are all children of God through faith. . . . There is no longer Jew or Greek, there is no longer slave or free, there is no longer male and female; for all of you are one in Christ Jesus." To the Romans, Paul listed and thanked twenty-eight outstanding leaders of the early churches, at least ten of whom were women:

> "I commend to you our sister Phoebe, a deacon of the church at Cenchreae. . . . Greet Prisca and Aquila, who work with me in Christ Jesus. . . . Greet Mary, who has worked very hard among you. Greet Andronicus and Junia, my relatives who were in prison with me; they are prominent among the apostles, and they were in Christ before I was. . . . Greet Philologus, Julia, Nereus and his sister, and Olympas, and all the saints who are with them."

It is inconceivable to me that Paul would encourage and congratulate inspired women who were successful deacons, apostles, ministers, and saints and still be quoted by modern male chauvinists as a biblical reason for excluding women from accepting God's call to serve others in the name of Christ. In reality, Paul has not separated himself from the lesson that Jesus taught: that women are to be treated equally in their right to serve God.

Devout Christians can find adequate Scripture to justify either side in this debate. The question is whether we evangelical believers in Christ want to abandon his example and exclude a vast array of potential female partners, who are equally devout and responding to God's call to serve with us in advancing God's kingdom on earth.

Women are greatly abused in many countries in the world, and the alleviation of their plight is made less likely by the mandated subservience of women by Christian fundamentalists. What is especially disappointing to me is the docile acceptance by so many strong Christian women of their subjugation and restricted role.

10

FUNDAMENTALISM
IN GOVERNMENT

Among America's senior political leaders there are other vivid examples of the threats to our country's basic constitutional separation of powers. Some of the more conservative officials in Washington demonstrated their frustration with the independence of the judiciary by injecting themselves at the last moment into the highly controversial Terri Schiavo case after nearly twenty judges, most of them conservative jurists appointed by Republicans, had maintained their fifteen-year refusal to extend her life artificially.

Making it clear that he was speaking as a heart surgeon, Senate Majority Leader Bill Frist pronounced to his colleagues that he condemned the judicial consensus, "based on a review of the video footage which I spent an hour or so looking at last night in my office here in the Capitol. And that footage, to me, depicted something very different than persistent vegetative state." This diagnosis contradicted the subsequent medical examiner's autopsy performed on Mrs. Schiavo, which reported that she was blind and her brain was "grossly abnormal," less than half its normal size.

Enraged with the judges, Republican House Majority Leader Tom DeLay issued threats of imposing legislative control over state and federal courts. He ordered a congressional investigation of the judges and made a series of irate proclamations: "Judicial independence does not equal judicial supremacy." "These [rulings] are not examples of a mature society, but of a judiciary run amok." He added, "Congress for many years has shirked its responsibility to hold the judiciary accountable. No longer. The response of the legislative branch has mostly been to complain. There is another way, ladies and gentlemen, and that is to reassert our constitutional authority over the courts." He also said, "We set up the courts. We can unset the courts. We have the power of the purse."

A number of bills were introduced in Congress to interfere directly in judicial affairs after the Supreme Court struck down the death penalty for children, failed to approve display of the Ten Commandments on public property, and issued a ruling concerning the execution of Mexican nationals in Texas. House Republicans introduced a resolution declaring that international law should not be taken into account in interpreting the Constitution, and a Senate bill would bar the federal courts from applying the First Amendment in matters of controversy concerning separation of church and state. One of the foundations of constitutional law is the *habeas corpus* power of the federal courts to determine whether an indigent defendant has been unjustly sentenced to death in state courts. There is a strong move in Congress to shift this power to the attorney general, America's chief prosecutor!

When a judge was killed in an Atlanta courtroom by an irate criminal and the mother and husband of a Chicago judge were assassinated because of a dismissed lawsuit, a Republican from Texas explained in the Senate chamber that frustration "builds up and builds up to the point" that violence occurs against judges who "are making political decisions yet are unaccountable to the public." Even though a former judge himself, he suggested that the limited role of the Supreme Court should be "an enforcer of political decisions made by elected representatives of the people." It was to avoid this kind of intimidation of the judiciary that our founding fathers separated the three branches of government, with federal judges appointed for life and broad support required for approval of new judicial appointees.

There is a close compatibility between this recent revolutionary pattern in our U.S. Congress and those chosen to serve in high executive offices. Some have been admired and trusted both here and abroad, but the appointment of others has created the opposite reaction. One of the most intriguing and illustrative cases has been an outspoken man named John Bolton, the early choice in 2001 for undersecretary of state for arms control. While I was leading a Carter Center delegation to Havana the following year, Bolton announced falsely that Cuba's pharmaceutical industry was involved in the production of biological weapons of mass destruction. The Cubans immediately offered to permit U.S. scientists to inspect the facilities, but there was no response from Washington. When he could not force intelligence analysts to corroborate his statements, Bolton attempted to have them discharged or transferred to other posts. This action epitomized the politicization by top policy makers of intelligence information, which led to the fiasco over incorrect claims that Iraq had massive arsenals of weapons of mass destruction.

Within the State Department, Bolton worked to reverse decades of U.S. nonproliferation and arms control policies, claiming that the system of arms treaties established since World War II — with agreements negotiated by all U.S. presidents from Dwight Eisenhower to George H. W. Bush — has constrained U.S. power and infringed on American sovereignty without commensurate benefits. This belief was, unfortunately, shared by his superiors in the White House and has been adopted as official American policy.

Bolton's publicly expressed philosophy and statements about the United Nations had long been a matter of concern or amusement, and his choice as our nation's ambassador to the United Nations was a shock to everyone who respects the institution and the purpose of its work during the past sixty years. Concerning compliance with existing international agreements, he expressed his views clearly: "It is a big mistake for us to grant any validity to international law even when it may seem in our short-term interest to do so — because, over the long term, the goal of those who think that international law really means anything are those who want to constrict the United States."

He has insisted that "the United Nations is valuable only when it directly serves the United States." When asked about negotiation as a way to resolve international disputes, he responded, "I don't do carrots."

Fifty-nine of America's most distinguished diplomats condemned his selection because of these well-known attitudes, but especially dwelled on his abysmal performance as our nation's senior arms control official. They said he had an "exceptional record" of *opposing* U.S. efforts to improve national security through arms control.

The troubling fact is that, in all these attitudes, Bolton has accurately represented the revolutionary new foreign policies of the United States. In response to the expression of concern by the diplomats, a group of incumbent and former Republican officials have stated, in fact, that critics of his opinions are "misdirected" because his views "are identical" to those of the president and that "their differences seem to be with a man twice elected by the American people to design and execute security policies, rather than with one of his most effective and articulate officials in advancing those policies." Unable to get Bolton's nomination confirmed by the Senate, President Bush sent him to the U.N. with a recess appointment.

The term "neoconservative," or "neocon," has become commonly used to describe those who have shaped our new government philosophy. A completely outdated but traditional dictionary meaning is "a former liberal who espouses a moderate political conservatism," or "a newcomer to conservatism." My first encounter with the appellation was when President Reagan's "neocon" ambassador to the United Nations, Jeane Kirkpatrick, denounced me as having attempted to "impose liberalization and democratization" on other countries. She derided "the belief that it is possible to democratize governments anytime, anywhere, under any circumstances." Democracy, she said, depends "on complex social, cultural, and economic conditions," and takes "decades, if not centuries." She went on to extol "traditional authoritarian dictatorships" like Nicaragua under Somoza, the Philippines under Marcos, and Chile under Pinochet. I remember that one of

Kirkpatrick's first diplomatic missions was to the dictators in Chile and Argentina to assure them that my intrusive human rights policy would no longer be a problem for them.

Since then, I have been confused about the definition of neoconservatives, who seem to have condemned the political policies of most other presidents, Democratic and Republican, and have not had permanent alliances with either liberals or conservatives. Although the definition is obviously complex and changeable, "neocons" now seem to embrace aggressive and unilateral intervention in foreign affairs, especially to advance U.S. military and political influence in the Middle East.

Some neocons now dominate the highest councils of government, seem determined to exert American dominance throughout the world, and approve of preemptive war as an acceptable avenue to reach this imperialistic goal. Eight years before he became vice president, Richard Cheney spelled out this premise in his "Defense Strategy for the 1990s." Either before or soon after 9/11, he and his close associates chose Iraq as the first major target, apparently to remove a threat to Israel and to have Iraq serve as our permanent military, economic, and political base in the Middle East.

This dependence on military force to expand America's influence and other recent deviations from traditional values have dramatically reduced the attractiveness of our political, cultural, and religious offerings to the world. Although most Americans are convinced of the superiority of these attributes of our Western society, it has become increasingly obvious that a heavy-handed effort to impose them on other people can be counterproductive.

Some of the "neocons" and historic spokespersons for conservative causes are now denouncing that designation entirely, claiming neither to be new conservatives nor to be associated with recent domestic and international government policies, including high deficits, intrusion of the federal government into state and individual affairs, and imperialistic adventures. I have chosen to use "fundamentalist" to describe a conglomeration of characteristics, some of them attributable to "neocons" or the extreme right wing, recognizing that there are no commonly accepted definitions of these descriptive words.

There are obviously sincere differences of opinion within the religious and political life of our nation, and this is to be expected. It is the unprecedented combined impact of fundamentalism in religion and politics that has helped to create the deep and increasingly disturbing divisions among our people. This is a basic challenge that the citizens of our country will have to meet and resolve, in order to shape the future heart and soul of America.

I am convinced that our great nation could realize all reasonable dreams of global influence if we properly utilized the advantageous values of our religious faith and historic ideals of peace, economic and political freedom, democracy, and human rights.

11

THE DISTORTION OF AMERICAN FOREIGN POLICY

Although there are many other complicating political factors, the tendency of fundamentalists to choose certain emotional issues for demagoguery and to avoid negotiation with dissenters has adversely affected American foreign policy. One notable example is that some American political leaders have adopted Fidel Castro as the ultimate human villain, and have elevated the small and militarily impotent nation of Cuba as one of the greatest threats to our nation's security and culture.

There was a justified concern, during a brief period more than four decades ago, when President John Kennedy was informed that Soviet missiles were being sent to Cuba, and the "Cuban missile crisis" was properly named. Since then, the continued fixation on Cuba has become ludicrous and counterproductive. A punitive embargo has been imposed on the already suffering Cuban people, the freedom of our own citizens to visit and trade with Cuba has been curtailed, and cultural and humanitarian cooperation has been outlawed. The only tangible results of this policy have been to hurt the people of Cuba, turn them against the United States, promote Castro's undeserved status as a small David successfully confronting the Goliath in Washington, perpetuate his political dictatorship, and deprive Americans of our own freedoms.

With the missile crisis resolved, in 1977 I removed all travel restraints so that unimpeded visitation by Cuban-Americans and others would result in extensive cordial encounters and friendships with the oppressed Cuban citizens and improve the likelihood of their demanding the freedoms guaranteed under their own constitution and laws. I also began the process of establishing diplomatic relations, approving "interest sections," or official delegations, in Washington and Havana. Responding to pressure from militant Cuban expatriates in Florida, my successors in office have reversed these decisions, except that the offices we established in Washington and

Havana have survived and serve, at least, as avenues of communication.

In 2002, I decided to accept an invitation from President Fidel Castro to visit his country, but only after he guaranteed me the right to speak directly and without censorship to the Cuban people, both on television and radio. I did so in my limited Spanish, acknowledging the benefits of Cuba's superior services in education and health but emphasizing how Cubans' freedom and political rights were being violated, and encouraging a strong and respected dissident movement known as the Varela Project. Oswaldo Payá Sardiñas, head of the Christian Liberation Movement, had obtained more than ten thousand signatures on a petition to be presented publicly to the Cuban parliament, demanding the rights of freedom prescribed in the nation's constitution. Since my visit, unfortunately, the White House has increasingly curtailed the freedom of American citizens to visit, communicate, or trade with Cubans, and there has been a predictable and commensurate crackdown on protesting voices in Cuba.

A typical example of the personal impact of these recent U.S. policies is the case of an American serviceman, Sergeant Carlos

Lazo, who has two teenage sons living in Cuba who do not wish to follow their father in emigrating to the United States. After returning from Iraq, where he participated in the especially ferocious and costly attack on Fallujah, the sergeant traveled to Miami and made a routine request to visit his sons. Under the new policy, he was denied permission and informed that such family visits will not be permitted, except possibly every three years. It is troubling to realize that American Sergeant Lazo could visit his sons if he were a citizen of any other nation in the world.

American policy toward our entire hemisphere has been misshaped by this obsession. It has become almost impossible for any career diplomat who does not demonstrate a near-fanatic commitment to the isolation of the Cuban people to acquire a high post in the State Department, and this philosophy permeates American embassies throughout the region.

For many years, The Carter Center has been deeply involved in Latin America in efforts to reduce suffering from diseases and to promote human rights and democratic governments; our activity has included the monitoring of many troubled elections. We are intimately familiar with the local political situation in a number of countries. The oppressive regime in Havana is still a notable and disturbing holdout against democratic reforms, but our government's distorted policies in other nations are causing a wave of anti-American sentiment and the overthrow and replacement of leaders who appear too closely tied to Washington.

Eight elected South American presidents who fit this description have been forced from office since 2000, and a wave of leftist leaders has been chosen, all the way from Chile and Argentina in the south to Venezuela in the north, including Ecuador, Brazil, and Bolivia. They now govern two-thirds of the continent. This reaction against American policy is likely to play a major role in forthcoming elections in other countries, including Mexico.

In May 2005, the candidate endorsed by Venezuela's President Hugo Chávez, José Miguel Insulza, a Chilean socialist, was elected secretary general of the Organization of American States, the first time a candidate was ever chosen who was not backed by the United States.

The Bush administration's obsession with the International Criminal Court (ICC) is an additional irritant. For several years, The Carter Center worked with Washington officials and leaders from many other nations to evolve the ICC, designed to prevent and punish acts of genocide and horrendous war crimes such as those in Rwanda, Yugoslavia, Cambodia, Sierra Leone, and Darfur, Sudan. The ICC charter, signed in 2002 by 139 nations, was carefully drafted to prevent punishment of Americans for genocidal acts overseas, provided U.S. courts will address any such crimes. However, the United States is now attempting to force subservient nations to guarantee blanket immunity for American military personnel, contractor employees, and tourists. In addition to countries in other regions, twelve Latin American and Caribbean countries are being deprived of military and other aid, arousing deep resentment and damaging their ability and willingness to cooperate with us regarding the control of narcotics, illegal immigration, and terrorism.

An aversion to negotiation with adversaries has shaped another sensitive, difficult, and dangerous issue in which I have been directly involved. In June 1994 the North Koreans had expelled inspectors of the International Atomic Energy Agency (IAEA) and were threatening to process spent fuel from an old graphite-moderated nuclear reactor in Yongbyon into plutonium. This could give them the capability to produce nuclear weapons. The threat of war was clear on the Korean peninsula as the United Nations Security Council was being urged by the United States to impose severe sanctions on North Korea.

There was a general consensus, shared by American military experts, that the combined forces of South Korea and the United States could defeat North Korea, but it was known that more than twenty thousand shells and missiles could be launched quickly by North Korea into nearby Seoul, South Korea. The American military commander in South Korea, General Gary Luck, estimated that total casualties would far exceed those of the previous Korean War.

Responding to several years of invitations from North Korean president Kim Il Sung and expressions of deep concern from Chinese leaders, and with the approval of President Bill Clinton, Rosalynn and I went to Pyongyang and helped to secure an agreement from President Kim that North Korea would cease its nuclear program at Yongbyon and permit IAEA inspectors to return to the site to assure that the spent fuel was not reprocessed. The North Korean leader also promised me that he would have full diplomatic discussions with South Korea's president, Kim Young Sam, who immediately accepted the invitation we delivered to him. Kim Il Sung died shortly thereafter, and it was only later that this promise of a summit conference was fulfilled by his son Kim Jong Il.

Following up on these commitments, the United States and our allies subsequently assured the North Koreans that there would be no military threat to them, that a supply of fuel oil would be substituted for power production lost when nuclear production was terminated at Yongbyon, and that two modern atomic power plants would be built, with their fuel rods and operation to be monitored by international inspectors.

The spent fuel at Yongbyon (estimated to be adequate for a half dozen or so bombs) continued to be monitored, but promised construction of the replacement nuclear plants was delayed. Extensive bilateral discussions were held between the United States and North Korea, and Secretary of State Madeleine Albright visited Pyongyang to resolve any difficulties.

With his election as president of South Korea, Kim Dae Jung initiated a strong effort to work with North Korean president Kim Jong Il to bring peace to the peninsula, and made enough progress to earn the 2000 Nobel Peace Prize.

With the advent of a new administration in Washington in 2001, the entire policy was changed dramatically. North Korea was publicly branded as part of an "axis of evil," with direct and implied threats of military action against the isolated and paranoid nation, and an official policy was established that prohibited any direct discussions with the North Koreans to resolve differences. Shipments of the pledged fuel oil were terminated, along with construction of the alternate nuclear power plants. Both Korean leaders and their ongoing north-south peace efforts were publicly ridiculed in an Oval Office summit meeting with South Korean president Kim Dae Jung.

Responding in its ill-advised but predictable way to this American policy, Pyongyang announced that it had withdrawn from the Non-Proliferation Treaty, expelled IAEA inspectors, resumed processing of the Yongbyon fuel rods, and was developing nuclear explosive devices. The United

States claimed that uranium was also being purified for possible weapons use, but Chinese and South Korean experts expressed doubts about the accuracy of this report. If true, these North Korean decisions to develop nuclear weapons are gross violations of previous agreements and a serious threat to peace and stability in the region.

The primary obstacles to progress are a peremptory United States demand that North Koreans renounce all nuclear activity and a decision that communication between our two countries will be accepted only within a six-nation forum, while Pyongyang leaders have insisted on resumption of direct bilateral discussions and a clear statement from Washington that American leaders have "no hostile intent" against them. North Korean officials announced in 2005 that they have refueled their nuclear reactor at Yongbyon once again, for the first time since 2002, giving them another eight thousand nuclear fuel rods that may be processed into explosive material.

Selig Harrison, who has visited North Korea nine times, most recently in April 2005, states that

"the ascendancy of the [Korean] hardliners is the direct result of the Bush administration's ideologically driven North Korea policy and can be reversed only if the United States makes a fresh start attuned to the conciliatory engagement approach now being pursued by South Korean President Roh Moo Hyun. . . . In any case, it is increasingly clear that the administration made a catastrophic blunder in December 2002 by abrogating the 1994 nuclear freeze, using the uranium accusation as its justification. This gave the hard-liners their rationale for resuming plutonium reprocessing, thus creating the present crisis."

Harrison quotes North Korea's chief negotiator, Kang Sok Ju, the same top official with whom I negotiated technical details in 1994, as saying that direct and secret talks to resolve the impasse could begin with a formal statement that the United States "will respect the sovereignty and territorial integrity of the Democratic People's Republic of Korea and is prepared for peaceful coexistence."

The basic military situation is similar but worse than it was a decade ago: we can destroy the entire nation with our massive military forces, but it is now likely that, with nuclear explosives, many more than a million South Korean and American casualties would result.

A recent announcement of withdrawal of U.S. troops farther away from the demilitarized zone has caused increasing concern in South Korea that hard-line leaders in Pyongyang and Washington might precipitate the threatened conflict. An April 2005 public opinion poll revealed that 29.5 percent of South Koreans consider the United States to be their greatest threat, compared with 18.4 percent who named North Korea. Among university students, 50.1 percent saw America as the major obstacle to peace in the peninsula.

Strong arguments can be made on both sides of this crucial issue, but good-faith diplomacy between the United States and North Korea is necessary. So far, a fundamentalist policy of not negotiating with those who disagree with us has backfired in North Korea, possibly resulting in the Communist regime's churning out nuclear weapons. At the same time, we have antagonized our Far East allies and diminished America's influence and stature in Asia. It is unlikely that the North Koreans will back down unless the United States meets their basic demands.

If America will negotiate as in the past, the simple framework for an agreement exists, with all elements being confirmed by mutual actions combined with unimpeded international inspections:

- The United States gives a firm statement of "no hostile intent" and moves toward normal relations if North Korea forgoes any nuclear weapons program and remains at peace with its neighbors.

- Basic premises of the agreements of 1994 are honored, with North Korea, Japan, South Korea, the United States, Russia, and China cooperating.

Another indication of this fundamentalist policy of not communicating with potential adversaries has been the recent U.S. approach to Syria. In order to promote peace in the Middle East and, on occasion, to comply with White House requests, Rosalynn and I first visited Damascus in 1983 and returned several times. We had long and often beneficial discussions with President Hafez al-Assad, and have had a chance to know his family. This includes his son, Bashar al-Assad, who succeeded his father as Syria's leader in June 2000.

With plans to go to the Middle East in July 2005 to observe the Palestinian elections, I arranged on the same trip to visit the leaders of Syria, Jordan, and Egypt. Syria had completed withdrawing its troops from Lebanon, and Egypt had announced plans for some form of democratic election. My goal was to pay my personal respects to the leaders and to discuss their changing domestic and international interests. I also wanted to encourage their support for the peace process between Israel and the Palestinians and to explore any helpful ideas or suggestions for our planned meetings with Palestinian leaders. An ancillary purpose was to obtain insights that might be helpful to me in writing my next book, in which I plan to cover developments in their region.

Two months in advance, as customary, I notified the State Department and the White House of my travel plans, and almost immediately received a call from the president's national security adviser. He informed me that Syria had not been cooperative in some issues involving the nearby war in Iraq, and that U.S. policy was to restrict all visits to Damascus as a means of putting pressure on President

Bashar al-Assad. After a somewhat heated discussion, he requested officially and on behalf of the president that our visit be canceled. This was an almost unprecedented experience for me, but I was forced to comply.

One of the most bizarre admixtures of religion and government is the strong influence of some Christian fundamentalists on U.S. policy in the Middle East. Almost everyone in America has heard of the *Left Behind* series, by Tim LaHaye and Jerry B. Jenkins, twelve books that have set all-time records in sales. Their religious premise is based on a careful selection of Bible verses, mostly from the book of Revelation, and describes the scenario for the end of the world. When the Messiah returns, true believers will be lifted into heaven, where, with God, they will observe the torture of most other humans who are left behind. This transcendent event will be instantaneous, and the timing unpredictable. There are literally millions of my fellow Baptists and others who believe every word of this vision, based on self-exaltation of the chosen few along with the condemnation and abandonment, during a period of "tribulation," of family members, friends, and neighbors who have not been chosen for salvation.

It is the injection of these beliefs into America's governmental policies that is a cause for concern. These believers are convinced that they have a personal responsibility to hasten this coming of the "rapture" in order to fulfill biblical prophecy. Their agenda calls for a war in the Middle East against Islam (Iraq?) and the taking of the entire Holy Land by Jews (occupation of the West Bank?), with the total expulsion of all Christians and other gentiles. This is to be followed by infidels (Antichrists) conquering the area, and a final triumph of the Messiah. At this time of rapture, all Jews will either be converted to Christianity or be burned.

Based on these premises, some top Christian leaders have been in the forefront of promoting the Iraqi war, and make frequent trips to Israel, to support it with funding, and lobby in Washington for the colonization of Palestinian territory. Strong pressure from the religious right has been a major factor in America's quiescent acceptance of the massive building of Israeli settlements and connecting highways on Palestinian territory in the West Bank. Some Israeli leaders have utilized this assistance while conveniently ignoring the predicted final plight of all Jews.

This has helped to bring about another dramatic departure from the American opposition to settlement activity that prevailed during the previous four decades, beginning when Dwight Eisenhower was president and extending through the terms of his successors, until 1993, when President Bill Clinton gave almost blanket approval to settlement expansion. President George H. W. Bush had been especially forceful in opposing specific Israeli settlements between Jerusalem and Bethlehem, even threatening to cut off financial assistance to Israel.

Although some encroachment on Palestinian territory can be accommodated in future peace negotiations, current Israeli plans to retain far-reaching West Bank settlements and to expand a large enclave known as Ma'aleh Adumim from deep within the West Bank all the way into East Jerusalem will likely spell the death knell for prospects for the "road map for peace," the keystone of President George W. Bush's Middle East policy. This will be a tragedy for the Israelis and the Palestinians.

12

ATTACKING TERRORISM, NOT HUMAN RIGHTS?

This is an especially unpleasant chapter to write, because it includes some embarrassing assessments of the government I have led and whose values I have defended. The concept that America maintains superior moral and ethical standards propelled us, immediately after the 9/11 attacks, into a global leadership role in combating terrorism. Our nation had long raised the banner of human rights for all others to see and follow, a role that has been described as a "self-assigned Messianic role in world affairs." To restore and then maintain these national values, it is important that Americans understand the revolutionary changes in policy that we are using to reach our crucial goal of self-protection.

I grew up in the Deep South, in a region where slavery had been a dominant factor of life for almost 250 years until abolished by ratification of the Fourteenth and Fifteenth Amendments to the U.S. Constitution in 1868 and 1870. During my boyhood, however, slavery had been replaced by racial segregation based on the U.S. Supreme Court's 1896 ruling that "separate but equal" treatment of black people was both legal and acceptable. With the political courage of President Harry Truman, the legal discrimination was eliminated in the U.S. armed forces in 1948, including the submarine in which I was serving, and then throughout our nation within the next two decades by the civil rights movement headed by Martin Luther King Jr. and the strong leadership of President Lyndon Johnson.

This triumph of civil rights at home did not preclude America's acceptance and support of some of the most brutal foreign regimes in our hemisphere and other regions, which blatantly violated the human rights of their own citizens. As a newly elected president, I announced that the protection of these rights would be the foundation of our country's foreign policy, and I persistently took action to implement this commitment. It has been gratifying to observe a wave of democratization sweep across our hemisphere and in other regions, as the fundamental rights of freedom were respected.

During the past four years there have been dramatic changes in our nation's policies toward protecting these rights. Many of our citizens have accepted these unprecedented policies because of the fear of terrorist attacks, but the damage to America's reputation has been extensive. Formerly admired almost universally as the preeminent champion of human rights, the United States now has become one of the foremost targets of respected international organizations concerned about these basic principles of democratic life. Some of our actions are similar to those of abusive regimes that we have historically condemned.

Following the attacks of 9/11, the U.S. government overreacted by detaining more than twelve hundred innocent men throughout America, none of whom were ever convicted of any crime related to terrorism. Their identities have been kept secret, and they were never given the right to hear charges against themselves or to have legal counsel. Almost all of them were Arabs or Muslims, and many have been forced to leave America.

To legalize such abuses of civil liberties, the Patriot Act was hurriedly enacted, with a number of temporary provisions scheduled to expire in 2005. Leading opponents of some of its provisions are very conservative and well-known Republicans who have organized groups known as Patriots to Restore Checks and Balances, and Free Congress Research and Education Foundation. The president has called for the law to be expanded and made permanent, but even the conservative "patriots" have deplored such provisions as authorization for federal agents to search people's homes and businesses secretly, to confiscate property without any deadline or without giving notice that the intrusion has taken place, and to collect without notice personal information on American citizens, including their medical histories, books checked out of libraries, and goods they purchase. The government can now seize an entire database — all the medical records of a hospital or all the files of an immigration group — when it is investigating a single person. Although most of the disputed sections of the Patriot Act are not focused on suspected terrorists but apply to the general public, government leaders have succeeded in having them extended or made permanent.

A large number of men and some young

boys have been captured in the wars in Afghanistan and Iraq and transferred to an American prison camp in Guantánamo, Cuba, where about 520 people from forty nations have been incarcerated and held incommunicado for more than three years, almost all without legal counsel and with no charges leveled against them. It has also been confirmed by U.S. officials that many have been physically abused.

After visiting six of the twenty-five or so U.S. prisons, the International Committee of the Red Cross reported registering 107 detainees under eighteen, some as young as eight years old. The journalist Seymour Hersh reported in May 2005 that Defense Secretary Donald Rumsfeld had received a report that there were "800–900 Pakistani boys 13–15 years of age in custody." The International Red Cross, Amnesty International, and the Pentagon have gathered substantial testimony of torture of children, confirmed by soldiers who witnessed or participated in the abuse. In addition to personal testimony from children about physical and mental mistreatment, a report from Brigadier General Janis Karpinski, formerly in charge of Abu Ghraib, described a visit to an eleven-year-old detainee in the cell block that housed high-risk prisoners.

The general recalled that the child was weeping, and "he told me he was almost twelve," and that "he really wanted to see his mother, could he please call his mother." Children like this eleven-year-old have been denied the right to see their parents, a lawyer, or anyone else, and were not told why they were detained. A Pentagon spokesman told Mr. Hersh that "age is not a determining factor in detention."

Physicians for Human Rights reported in April 2005 that "at least since 2002, the United States has been engaged in systematic psychological torture" of Guantánamo detainees that has "led to devastating health consequences for the individuals subjected to" it. The prisoners' outlook on life was not improved when the Secretary of Defense declared that most of them would not be released even if they were someday tried and found to be innocent.

Dr. Burton J. Lee III, President George H. W. Bush's personal White House physician, issued this statement:

"Reports of torture by U.S. forces have been accompanied by evidence that military medical personnel have played a role in this abuse and by new military ethical guidelines that in effect authorize complicity by health professionals in ill-treatment of detainees. These new guidelines distort traditional ethical rules beyond recognition to serve the interests of interrogators, not doctors and detainees. . . . Systematic torture, sanctioned by the government and aided and abetted by our own profession, is not acceptable. As health professionals, we should support the growing calls for an independent, bipartisan commission to investigate torture in Iraq, Afghanistan, Guantánamo Bay and elsewhere, and demand restoration of ethical standards that protect physicians, nurses, medics and psychologists from becoming facilitators of abuse. America cannot continue down this road. Torture demonstrates weakness, not strength. It does not show understanding, power or magnanimity. It is not leadership. It is a reaction of government officials overwhelmed by fear who succumb to conduct unworthy of them and of the citizens of the United States."

The terrible pictures from Abu Ghraib prison in Iraq have brought discredit on our country. This is especially disturbing, since U.S. intelligence officers estimated to the Red Cross that 70 to 90 percent of the detainees at this prison were held by mistake. Military officials reported that at least 108 prisoners have died in American custody in Iraq, Afghanistan, and other secret locations just since 2002, with homicide acknowledged as the cause of death in at least 28 cases. The fact that only one of these was in Abu Ghraib prison indicates the widespread pattern of prisoner abuse, certainly not limited to the actions or decisions of just a few rogue enlisted persons.

Iraqi major general Abed Hamed Mowhoush reported voluntarily to American officials in Baghdad in an attempt to locate his sons, and was detained, tortured, and stuffed inside a green sleeping bag, where he died from trauma and suffocation on November 26, 2003.

The superficial investigations under the auspices of the Department of Defense have made it obvious that no high-level military officers or government officials will be held accountable, but there is no doubt that their public statements and private directives cast doubt and sometimes ridicule on the applicability of international standards of human rights and the treatment of prisoners.

In November 2003 and again in June

2005, deeply concerned about the adverse impact of these new U.S. policies in other nations, The Carter Center hosted leading defenders of human rights and democracy movements from several dozen countries. My cochairs at both conferences were the U.N. High Commissioners for Human Rights, and other international human rights organizations played a key role in the discussions.

What we learned in these sessions was quite disturbing, the reports coming from courageous and effective nonviolent activists who take great risks in dangerous circumstances to protect freedom and the rights of others. Many of them had been either imprisoned or severely harassed as a result of holding their governments accountable to international standards of human rights and the principles of democracy. They were convinced that there had been a high-level, broad-based, and deliberate change in U.S. policy, abandoning or lowering our long-standing commitment to protect fundamental human rights within our nation and throughout the world. The human rights defenders also reported in 2003 that a large number of accused persons were being sent from America to selected foreign countries where torture was acceptable as a means of extracting information. This allegation was strongly denied by officials who represented the U.S. government at this conference.

The participants were in broad agreement that recent policies of the United States were being adopted and distorted by opportunistic regimes to serve their own interests. They told of a general retreat by their governments from previous human rights commitments, and emphasized that there was a danger of setting back democratic movements by decades in some of their countries. Participants explained that oppressive leaders had been emboldened to persecute and silence outspoken citizens under the guise of fighting terrorism, and that this excuse was deflecting pressure coming from the United States and other powers regarding human rights violations. The consequence was that many lawyers, professors, doctors, and journalists had been labeled terrorists, often for merely criticizing a particular policy or for carrying out their daily work. We heard about many cases involving human rights attorneys being charged with abetting terrorists simply for defending accused persons.

Equally disturbing were reports that the United States government is in some cases contributing directly to an erosion of human rights protection by encouraging governments to adopt regressive counterterrorism policies that lead to the undermining of democratic principles and the rule of law, often going far beyond the U.S. Patriot Act.

We all were encouraged because the most onerous of the new U.S. policies were being questioned in the Congress and through the federal court system and would ultimately be corrected. Although many legal issues had not yet reached the final appellate level to be clarified, most contested domestic cases had been resolved favorably, and the United States Supreme Court ruled in June 2004 that U.S. federal courts "have jurisdiction to consider challenges to the legality of the detentions of foreign nationals captured abroad in connection with hostilities and incarcerated at Guantánamo Bay."

While none of the Guantánamo detainees has yet obtained such a review because of government intransigence, a small number of them have been visited by lawyers seeking to file *habeas corpus* appeals. The U.S. administration has minimized compliance with the Supreme Court decision by establishing combatant status review tribunals (CSRT) to determine if a detainee is an "enemy combatant." Each CSRT is a panel of three military officers, ostensibly relying on secret evidence, to determine if the label "enemy combatant" should remain attached to each detainee, who still has no access to legal counsel to assist him. It took two and a half years after the detainees arrived there, but the decision was the first step toward forcing the administration to restore the rule of law in our dealings with foreigners in American custody.

In most of the countries represented at our human rights conferences, including young democracies, such checks and balances in the judicial system are not so well developed and make the questioning and reversal of abusive policies much less likely.

Another subject of concern among those who came from Northern Ireland, Turkey, Burma, Colombia, Israel, the occupied Palestinian territories, Uzbekistan, and other conflict-ridden societies was that the early use of military force and an announced policy of preemptive war sent a signal that violence had become a much more acceptable alternative to peaceful negotiations in the resolution of differences. The general consensus of these experts on democracy and freedom was that policies based on violence always result in a cycle of escalated violence.

It is apparent that prisoners of war are among the most vulnerable of people. Not only are they completely under the control of their captors, but in a time of conflict, the hatred and brutality of the battlefield are very likely to be mirrored within military prison walls. Other well-known factors are that wartime secrecy often cloaks the orders and policies of superiors and the actions of subordinates, and some elements of national hatred and fear are elevated by the psychology of war.

My own family experienced the impact of these factors when my favorite uncle, navy petty officer Tom Gordy, was brutally treated as a prisoner of war after being captured in Guam by the Japanese within a month of the attack on Pearl Harbor in 1941. After two years he was reported to be dead but was found after Japan's surrender, weighing eighty-five pounds, debilitated by four years of physical and psychological mistreatment.

The prevalence of such abuse of captured servicemen and -women during World War II induced the community of nations to come together to define quite precisely the basic guarantees of proper treatment for prisoners. These restraints are the result of an international conference held in Geneva, Switzerland, in 1949, and redefined and expanded what are known as the "Geneva Conventions." The authenticity and universal applicability of these guarantees were never questioned by a democratic power — until recently, and by America! Instead of honoring the historic restraints, our political leaders decided to violate them, using the excuse that we are at war against terrorism. It is obvious that the Geneva Conventions were designed specifically to protect prisoners of war, not prisoners of peace.

Although successful efforts by top officials have ensured that accountability and punishment will be limited to a few low-level military personnel, the basic changes in human rights policies were discussed and adopted in the White House, the Justice Department, and the Department of Defense — with spasmodic dissent from the State Department. Reports have revealed these kinds of official declarations:

"The president, despite domestic and international laws constraining the use of torture, has the authority as Commander in Chief to approve almost any physical or psychological actions during interroga-

tion, up to and including torture."
Department of Defense

"In my judgment, this new [post 9/11] paradigm renders obsolete Geneva's strict limitations on questioning of enemy prisoners and renders quaint some of its provisions."
White House legal counsel Alberto Gonzales, now Attorney General, the chief law enforcement officer of the United States

Subsequent evidence revealed that despite previous denials at our first human rights conference, American leaders had adopted a supplementary policy of transferring prisoners to foreign countries, including Egypt, Saudi Arabia, Syria, Morocco, Jordan, and Uzbekistan, most of which have been condemned in our government's annual human rights reports for habitually using torture to extract information. Although opposed by the State Department, this practice has been approved at the top levels of U.S. government. It is known as "extraordinary rendition," and the official excuses are that the victims have been classified as "illegal enemy combatants" and that our military or CIA personnel "don't know for certain" that they will be tortured. Members of Congress and legal specialists estimate that 150 prisoners have been included in this exceptional program. The techniques of torture are almost indescribably terrible, including, as a U.S. ambassador to one of the recipient countries reported, "partial boiling of a hand or an arm," with at least two prisoners boiled to death.

Of the many cases, one of the few that has been publicized involves the capture of a Canadian citizen, Maher Arar, when he was changing planes at Kennedy Airport in New York. He was shackled, loaded by U.S. agents into a Gulfstream 5 corporate jet, and taken to Syria, where he was abused for a year before being released after no evidence was found against him. U.S. officials knew what was happening. As the State Department had stated earlier about human rights abuses in Syria, "Former prisoners and detainees have reported that torture methods include electrical shocks, pulling out fingernails, the forced insertion of objects into the rectum, beatings, sometimes while the victim is suspended from the ceiling, hyperextension of the spine, and the use of a chair that bends backwards to asphyxiate the victim or fracture the spine."

Aside from the humanitarian aspects, it is well known that, under excruciating torture, a prisoner will admit almost any suggested crime. Such confessions are, of course, not admissible in trials in civilized nations. The primary goal of torture or the threat of torture is not to obtain convictions for crimes, but to engender and maintain fear. Some of our leaders have found that it is easy to forgo human rights for those who are considered to be subhuman, or "enemy combatants."

Again quoting America's new attorney general, Alberto Gonzales, the policy "places a high premium on . . . the ability to quickly obtain information from captured terrorists and their sponsors in order to avoid further atrocities against American civilians." He justifies an extension of the program permitting CIA agents to deal with suspects in foreign prison sites by claiming that the ban of the U.N. Convention Against Torture and Other Cruel, Inhuman, or Degrading Treatment or Punishment does not apply to American interrogations of foreigners overseas. According to him, the prisoners can be held indefinitely without any legal process and without access by the International Red Cross, even though the

United States has ratified international agreements that prohibit such treatment. The *New York Times* reports that a still-secret directive authorizing this policy was issued by President Bush in 2001. He also announced that members of Al-Qaeda and the Taliban were not entitled to prisoner-of-war status.

One serious consequence of this abominable procedure is the question of what to do with the tortured prisoners when they are proven innocent. Can they be released and free to give public testimony against the United States of America or even file lawsuits against our country, as a few of them have already done? Even if held in prison, some of them have become special problems because high-profile terrorists who were actually involved in the 9/11 attack have asked for them to be witnesses. Trials of these known criminals have been held in abeyance because we cannot afford to let the former or still-incarcerated detainees testify.

Instead of our correcting the basic problem, more and more prisoners are being retained, and there is less access to the facts about their treatment. A report released in March 2005 by Human Rights First said that the number of detainees in

U.S. custody in Iraq and Afghanistan has grown, just during the preceding six months, from six thousand to more than eleven thousand, and that the level of secrecy surrounding American detention operations has intensified.

As public scrutiny has been focused on the abuse of prisoners, historic reporting of CIA activities to Congress has been restricted to a tiny group of legislators. The law requires that the House and Senate Intelligence Committees be notified of all such activities, but the White House has claimed that the secret detention program is too sensitive, and is to be revealed only to the top Republican and Democrat on each panel. Predictably, other committee members have complained about their exclusion, but their ability to challenge policy lies only with the threat to withhold funding — not a desirable action when national security is the issue.

Republican Senator John McCain, who was a prisoner of war in Vietnam, has criticized the way detainees have been treated by U.S. forces, and he, Armed Forces Committee Chairman John Warner, and other Republican senators have proposed legislation that would prohibit the U.S. military from engaging in "cruel, inhuman or degrading treatment or punishment" of detainees, or from hiding prisoners from the Red Cross, and would set uniform standards for interrogating anyone detained by the Defense Department. These powerful Republican senators have quoted comments from fifteen top-ranking military officers: "The abuse of prisoners hurts America's cause in the war on terror, endangers U.S. service members who might be captured by the enemy, and is anathema to the values Americans have held dear for generations." McCain said, "The enemy we fight has no respect for human life or human rights. They don't deserve our sympathy. But this isn't about who they are. This is about who we are."

Representing the Bush administration, Vice President Cheney has made strenuous efforts to block the legislation, and the White House has warned that the $442 billion defense bill would be vetoed, claiming that it "would restrict the president's authority to protect Americans effectively from terrorist attack and bring terrorists to justice." However, under pressure, the White House announced in August 2005 that a large number of the prisoners at Guantánamo would be transferred to Afghanistan, Saudi Arabia, Yemen, and other Muslim nations where congressional scrutiny would not be so intense.

As our nation was being founded, George Washington decided to establish in America an innovative "policy of humanity." In 2003 I wrote a novel about our Revolutionary War, after six years of study and research. One of my most shocking discoveries was that British officers often ordered that "no quarter be granted" to Americans who surrendered on the battlefield. They were to be summarily executed. A vivid example of this was in the battle of Briar Creek, in northeast Georgia, when this order was given along with clear instructions that any British soldier who took a prisoner alive would be deprived of his rum ration for a month. General Washington condemned the practice and announced a more enlightened approach to warfare. Even though some American revolutionaries were later guilty of the same brutality, they were in violation of absolutely clear directives from their top commander.

It is an embarrassing tragedy to see a departure from our nation's historic leadership as a champion of human rights, with the abandonment defended legally by top officials. Only the American people can redirect our government's legal, religious, and political commitments to these ancient and unchanging moral principles.

13

PROTECTING OUR ARSENALS, BUT PROMOTING PROLIFERATION

There is a special international agreement that is designed to address the challenge of maintaining minimal nuclear arsenals and constraining proliferation: the Nuclear Non-Proliferation Treaty (NPT). It was first approved in 1970, and a total of 187 nations have now agreed to accept its terms, including the five major powers that first had nuclear arsenals. Its objective is "to prevent the spread of nuclear weapons and weapons technology, to promote cooperation in the peaceful uses of nuclear energy, and to further the goal of achieving nuclear disarmament and general and complete disarmament." This is the only binding commitment on non-proliferation between the nuclear weapon states and the nations that do not have nuclear weapons.

As a confidence-building measure, the

treaty established a safeguards system under the responsibility of the International Atomic Energy Agency (IAEA), which has power to conduct inspections of nuclear facilities within the signatory nations. The treaty promotes cooperation in the sharing of peaceful nuclear technology while providing safeguards to prevent the improper diversion of fissile material for weapons use. One of its main provisions is a review of the operation of the treaty every five years, and we have helped to convene meetings at The Carter Center prior to these anniversary dates to prepare for the formal conferences at the United Nations. As of the conference in 2005, only Israel, North Korea, India, and Pakistan were not participating. Three of these nations are known to have nuclear arsenals, and North Korea may have untested explosives.

There are now almost 30,000 nuclear weapons worldwide, of which the United States possesses about 12,000, Russia 16,000, China 400, France 350, Israel 200, Britain 185, and India and Pakistan 40 each. It is believed that North Korea has enough enriched nuclear fuel for a half dozen weapons.

The Non-Proliferation Treaty provides the major forum within which the world of nations attempts to minimize the nuclear threat, but because of decisions of the U.S. president and a few other national leaders, serious doubt has been cast on the future of the NPT itself. A recent United Nations report starkly warned: "We are approaching a point at which the erosion of the non-proliferation regime could become irreversible and result in a cascade of proliferation."

In rejecting or evading almost all nuclear arms control agreements negotiated during the past fifty years, the United States has now become the prime culprit in global nuclear proliferation. Former secretary of defense Robert McNamara summed up his concerns in the May/June 2005 issue of *Foreign Policy* magazine: "I would characterize current U.S. nuclear weapons policy as immoral, illegal, militarily unnecessary and dreadfully dangerous."

The signers of the treaty, including Iran, who do not have nuclear weapons insist that the 1970 treaty allows them to build nuclear facilities as long as they are for peaceful purposes. The International Atomic Energy Agency has the responsibility to inspect those sites to assure that they are not devoted to weapons production. There is a large group of "middle states," all of which have the resources and technical capability of developing nuclear weapons but have chosen to refrain from joining this exclusive "club."

The group includes Brazil, Egypt, Ireland, Mexico, New Zealand, South Africa, Sweden, and eight NATO members, and at The Carter Center, to prepare for the 2005 conference, they expressed a primary goal: "to exert leverage on the nuclear powers to take necessary steps to save the non-proliferation treaty." They contend that the United States and some other nuclear powers are not living up to their obligation to constrain or reduce their arsenals. This stalemate continues, with the additional demand that the Israeli arsenal be considered. When this coalition of nuclear-capable states introduced a proposal that called merely for the implementation of NPT commitments already made, the United States led Britain and France in voting against the resolution.

A proposal by the International Atomic Energy Agency would impose a five-year moratorium on all new enrichment of uranium and reprocessing of plutonium, the two normal paths to nuclear weapons, but the United States has joined Iran in opposing the moratorium because of its "potential disruption of nuclear power projects."

Despite the importance of the issues, neither the president, the secretary of state, nor any of their top deputies attended the 2005 conference in New York. With no senior officials there, the United States avoided subjecting our government to a debate about whether it is in compliance with its own obligations under the treaty.

One of the nuclear proliferation challenges that I faced as president was from India, which sought to obtain nuclear materials and advanced technology for their "civilian nuclear power program" without complying with the non-proliferation treaty. Despite otherwise friendly relations, I rejected this request. After I left office, India was able to proceed with their plans and conducted nuclear test explosions in 1998. The key inducement for NPT membership is that those in compliance will have exclusive access to highly sensitive nuclear technology. As a further move that weakened the non-proliferation effort, President Bush has announced plans to lift these restrictions and grant this privilege to India, which has rejected the NPT. This is a clear incitement for other nations to violate the treaty's restraints.

While claiming to be protecting the world from proliferation threats in Iraq,

Libya, Iran, and North Korea, American leaders have not only abandoned existing treaty restrictions but also assert plans to test and develop new weapons, including antiballistic missiles, the earth-penetrating "bunker buster," and perhaps some secret new "small" bombs. They have also reneged on past pledges and have reversed another long-standing policy, by threatening first use of nuclear weapons against nonnuclear states.

After rejecting restraints previously imposed by the Anti-Ballistic Missile Treaty, the United States has already spent more than $80 billion on "Star Wars," an ill-justified and wasteful effort to intercept and destroy an incoming intercontinental missile attack, and the costs continue at about $9 billion each year. There are three potential plans that have been assessed: to destroy an enemy missile immediately after takeoff, just before it strikes an American city, or somewhere during its flight (presumably from China, North Korea, or Russia). An attacker would be detected by space-based satellite monitors, by a massive radar installation in the Aleutian Islands of Alaska, or on a large floating platform at sea. In addition, interceptor techniques have been seriously assessed that use powerful laser beams on aircraft or missiles in hardened concrete land-based silos surrounding key U.S. cities for late-flight interception or in Alaska or other locations for midflight interception.

These Rube Goldberg efforts to deploy an antimissile system have been strongly supported by powerful military-industrial political forces and by a few true believers who are convinced that any defense effort, no matter how costly or infeasible, is justified — whether during the Cold War with the Soviets or, in more recent times, against terrorist attacks. In any case, they claim, our publicized efforts will intimidate adversaries. The overwhelming opinion of scientists and responsible and unbiased military experts is that the basic assumptions and priorities are wrong.

Repeated interception tests by the U.S. military have failed, even when our officials have known exactly when a test warhead was to be launched and what its trajectory would be. These are the simplest possible circumstances, although it is well known that any real attack would be without warning and the warhead would be accompanied by multiple decoys that would divert our interceptors.

In any case, it is extremely unlikely that

a poor developing country could design, develop, test, and deploy both nuclear warheads and intercontinental missiles to deliver the weapons without the entire world becoming aware of this capability. A much simpler technology would be to place a warhead on a short-range rocket or cruise missile and fire it from a few hundred miles offshore. There are hundreds of such vehicles available on the international market, including Iraq's highly publicized Scud missiles. In either of these scenarios, the attacker would most likely be identified — and destroyed.

It is even easier for a rogue nation or organization to make a small, dirty nuclear, chemical, or biological weapon and smuggle it undetected into the harbor at New York or any other major American seaport in a cargo container or in one of the dozens of ships that enter each week with no serious inspection. Such a weapon could also be loaded into a truck and hauled to an inland city before detonation. The identity of the attacker might be difficult or impossible to ascertain.

The unjustified expenditure of resources and the misapplication of priorities seem foolhardy, but the global consequences are much more serious. When American leaders gave the official announcement to Russia in 2001 that we would pull out of the ABM Treaty, it was predictable that Russia would respond by announcing plans to upgrade its nuclear forces without regard to existing arms control treaties.

The end of America's "no first use" nuclear weapons policy has aroused a somewhat predictable response in other nations. Chinese major general Zhu Chenghu announced in July 2005 that China's government was under internal pressure to change its "no first use" policy. "If the Americans draw their missiles and position-guided ammunition on to the target zone on China's territory, I think we will have to respond with nuclear weapons."

Until recently, all American presidents since Dwight Eisenhower have striven to restrict and reduce nuclear arsenals — some more than others. So far as I know, there are no present efforts by any of the nuclear powers to accomplish these crucial objectives, with mandatory goals and verification. The world is crying out for positive leadership from Washington, and there are some important steps that could be taken.

It should be remembered that the enormous nuclear arsenals of the United States and Russia still exist, and little bilateral effort has been made to reduce these unnecessary weapons, with mandatory verification of such agreements and the dismantling and disposal of decommissioned weapons. With massive arsenals still on hair-trigger alert, a global holocaust is just as possible now, through mistakes or misjudgments, as it was during the depths of the Cold War.

The Russians retain vast stockpiles of nuclear weapons and refined materials for the building of others. Rogue states or terrorists would take any steps to obtain these loosely guarded and valuable products. In 1991, U.S. senators Sam Nunn and Richard Lugar sponsored legislation that helped finance commitments by the United States and Russia to join in the proper disposal of these stockpiles, but this wise and effective program is in danger because of a recent lack of adequate financing and the inability of the two governments to agree on access to Russian sites and liability if anything goes wrong.

There is also an important opportunity for progress within NATO, which needs to deemphasize the role of its nuclear weapons and consider an end to their deployment in Western Europe. Despite its dramatic eastward expansion, NATO is retaining the same stockpiles and policies it had when the Iron Curtain divided the continent and many of its new members were potential targets for our nuclear missiles.

Another historic international commitment that is being abandoned is limitation on the further testing of existing nuclear weapons and the development of new ones. In August 1957, President Eisenhower announced a proposal to ban the further testing of nuclear explosives, and faltering progress has been made since that time. While I was president, there were strict global limits on the testing of any explosive above 150 kilotons, which at that time was the smallest that could be monitored. Subsequently, it became technologically feasible to detect very small explosions, and a Comprehensive Nuclear Test Ban Treaty was evolved. It has been signed and ratified by Russia, France, and the United Kingdom, and signed but not ratified by China and the United States. Although President Bill Clinton signed the treaty and pledged that it would not be violated, the most recent American budget refers, for the first time, to a list of possible U.S. tests that would violate the treaty.

Another radical shift in policy that

causes concern even among our closest allies is America's move toward deployment of destructive weapons in space. The ABM Treaty prohibited space-based weapons, but our government's abandonment of the treaty in 2002 opened the door to this extremely destabilizing project. The new Defense Department doctrine defines our goal as "freedom to attack as well as freedom from attack" in space. The goal is to strike any target on earth within forty-five minutes. As described by the U.S. Air Force, one method, named "Rods from God," would hurl cylinders of heavy metals to strike a target at seventy-two hundred miles per hour, with the destructive force of a small nuclear weapon. Although no official presidential directive has been revealed, the Pentagon has already spent billions of dollars developing such weapons and planning for their deployment. The government announced plans in June 2005 to begin production of plutonium-238, a highly radioactive material that is used almost exclusively as a power source for space vehicles.

There is little doubt that a global treaty to ban space weapons will leave America safer than a unilateral decision to put the first (and certainly not the only) weapons in space.

Even within our government, sharp disagreements have been revealed about what should be done with some of the key components of our aging nuclear inventory. Among approximately five thousand active warheads known to be in our nation's arsenal, the key weapon now deployed on submarines is called the W76, about which I was thoroughly briefed as president. It was designed during the Cold War to be as small and powerful as possible, within a thin and fragile case. The current argument is whether to refurbish the aging warheads or replace them with a new model. In addressing this issue, there will be great pressure to renounce completely the global ban on nuclear testing, precipitating a new arms race as other nations would almost certainly take the same action.

Nuclear proliferation is an increasing source of instability in the Middle East and in Asia. Iran has repeatedly hidden its intentions to enrich uranium while claiming that its nuclear program is for peaceful purposes only. This explanation has been given before, by India, Pakistan, and North Korea, and has led to weapons programs in all three nations. As Iran moves down the same path, direct diplomatic effort by the United States with an "axis of evil" nation is inconceivable. American leaders must rely on European intermediaries and threats of military action, with implications of support if Israel were to strike at Iran's nuclear facilities.

At the same time, Israel's uncontrolled and unmonitored weapons status entices leaders in neighboring Iran, Syria, Egypt, and other Arab nations to join the nuclear weapon community.

The fact is that the global threat of proliferation exists, and the destructive actions of several nonnuclear nations — and perhaps even some terrorist groups — will depend on lack of leadership among those who already have powerful arsenals but are not willing to restrain themselves. Like it or not, America is at the forefront in making this great moral decision. Instead of setting an example for others, we seem to be choosing proliferation.

14

WORSHIPING THE PRINCE OF PEACE, OR PREEMPTIVE WAR?

For months after the terrible terrorist attack in 2001, the American people were inundated almost daily with claims from top government officials that we faced a devastating threat from Iraq's weapons of mass destruction or from large and well-organized cadres of terrorists hiding in our country. But as was emphasized vigorously by foreign allies and key members of our own intelligence services, there was never any existing danger to the United States from Baghdad. It was obvious that with the U.N. sanctions, intense weapons inspections, and overwhelming American military superiority, any belligerent move by Saddam Hussein against a neighbor, an overt display of a weapon of mass destruction, or sharing of such technology with terrorist organizations would have been suicidal for Iraq. Iraq's weapons programs had already been reduced to impotence before the war was launched to eliminate them.

If Saddam Hussein had actually possessed a large nuclear, biological, or chemical arsenal, then the American invasion would have resulted in hundreds of thousands of casualties, many of them U.S. troops. There is no evidence that British or American leaders really expected or prepared for this eventuality. We cannot ignore the development of such weapons in any potential enemy nation or organization, but unilateral military action based on erroneous or deliberately distorted intelligence is not the answer.

Even as a small boy, my ambition was to go to the U.S. Naval Academy in Annapolis, to become a naval officer, and to devote my life's career to the defense of my country and its principles around the world. I left the navy's Reserve Officer Training Corps for Annapolis in 1943 and continued this professional service until I resigned my commission in 1953. Except for General Dwight Eisenhower, I spent more years in active military service than any other president since those who had served as generals in the War Between the States. Although prepared to give my life if necessary as a submarine officer, I joined other officers and men in a common commitment that America's obvious strength and steadfastness would be a deterrent to war — that we were the ones who were preserving peace. I never felt that my dedication to military service was a violation of my faith in Jesus Christ, the Prince of Peace.

Later, as president during the Cold War with the Soviet Union, I was faced with the truly awesome responsibility of protecting my nation and its global interests. Aware that I was playing the key role in an intense competition between freedom and communism in almost every corner of the world, I realized that any misstep could precipitate a nuclear holocaust. In addition to our long-range bombers and formidable land-based intercontinental missiles, we had developed a fleet of submarines that were constantly deployed at sea and almost impervious to any Soviet preemptive attack. With multiple warheads on the missiles of a single ship, we could have destroyed every major city in the entire Soviet Union.

One of the facts that I had to accept from my first day in office was that enemy intercontinental nuclear warheads, once launched, would require only twenty-six minutes to reach Washington, New York, and other American targets. During this brief interval, it was my sole responsibility as commander in chief to decide on our response.

There has never been any effective means of destroying an incoming intercontinental missile, and the Anti-Ballistic Missile Treaty between the nuclear weapon states specifically prevented attempts to develop such a defense. Under those circumstances, the only options were to launch a counterattack or to accept the horrible damage without response. My choice, obviously, was to avoid the possibility of this scenario, known by the appropriate acronym "MAD" (mutual assured destruction), by convincing the Soviets of our ability and resolve to respond, and through effective diplomacy to preserve the peace and protect American interests.

I have cherished a plaque that a cabinet member gave me the day I left office, with a quote from Thomas Jefferson:

I HAVE THE CONSOLATION TO REFLECT THAT DURING THE PERIOD OF MY ADMINISTRATION NOT A DROP OF THE BLOOD OF A SINGLE CITIZEN WAS SHED BY THE SWORD OF WAR

As I described in the previous chapter, current U.S. policy is threatening the effectiveness of international agreements that have been laboriously negotiated by almost all previous presidents. Perhaps even more disturbing as a threat to the maintenance of global stability is the unprecedented adoption of a policy of preemptive war. This recent decision is not only a radical departure from historic policies of the United States but also a violation of international laws that we have pledged to honor. The United Nations Charter grants to sovereign nations the inherent right of individual or collective self-defense, but only in the event of armed attack. Ignoring even our closest allies, our president has announced a decision that the United States would act as a law unto ourselves and launch preemptive military attacks, while rejecting the standard of "war as a last resort."

Daniel Webster (who four years later would be named secretary of state) in 1837 said that there must be "a necessity of self-defense . . . instant, overwhelming, leaving no choice of means, and no moment for deliberation." Former secretary of state Henry Kissinger, usually a strong supporter of Republican administrations, acknowledged that a policy of preemptive war is revolutionary and "challenges the international system."

Branding other nations as comprising an "axis of evil" marked them as potential targets and at the same time closed the usual doors of resolving bilateral differences with them through diplomatic means. Of more immediate and serious concern, the adoption of this radical policy frittered away the almost unanimous sympathy and pledges of support that came to us after the terrorist attack in 2001, now leaving us relatively alone in our long-term and crucial effort to contain and reduce the threat of terrorism.

It became apparent soon after the presidential election in 2000 that some of our new political leaders were determined to attack Iraq. With false and distorted claims after 9/11, they misled the U.S. Congress and the American public into believing that Saddam Hussein had somehow been responsible for the dastardly attack on the World Trade Towers and the Pentagon, and that Iraq was developing nuclear weapons and other mass destruction devices and posed a direct threat to the security of America.

Although the deceptiveness of these

statements was later revealed, the die was cast, and most of our trusting citizens were supportive of the war. Exaggerated claims of catastrophe from nonexistent weapons of mass destruction kept the fears alive, with Vice President Dick Cheney repeatedly making false statements, such as, "Instead of losing thousands of lives, we might lose tens of thousands, or even hundreds of thousands of lives in a single day of war." National Security Adviser Condoleezza Rice backed him with horrifying references to mushroom clouds over the cities of America, and Secretary of State Colin Powell went to the United Nations to make a conglomeration of inaccurate statements to the world. The administration later claimed that its information was erroneous, but intelligence sources were rewarded, not chastised.

There is little wonder that, at least for a few months, fearful American citizens and members of Congress supported the unnecessary war despite our nation's historic policy of relying on diplomacy instead of conflict to resolve disputes and despite the commitment of Christians to worship Jesus Christ as the Prince of Peace. For me personally and for most other Americans, this commitment to peace and diplomacy does not imply a blind or total pacifism. There are times when war is justified, and for many centuries the moral criteria for violence have been carefully delineated.

As it became more and more evident that our leaders were going to attack Iraq, I decided to write an essay for the *New York Times* that spelled out the minimal requirements for going to war. I used the same basic arguments with which Christian leaders (such as Saint Augustine around 400 A.D. and Saint Thomas Aquinas in the thirteenth century) had addressed this question quite clearly for at least sixteen hundred years, all basing their opinions on New Testament Scripture.

Not realizing that the top leaders of the United States and Great Britain had already agreed to invade Iraq almost a year earlier, I wrote these words for an op-ed piece on March 3, 2003:

"Just War, or an Unjust War?

"Profound changes have been taking place in American foreign policy, reversing consistent bi-partisan commitments that for more than two centuries have earned our nation's greatness. These have been predicated on basic religious principles, respect for international law, and alliances that resulted in wise decisions and mutual restraint. Our apparent determination to launch a war against Iraq, without international support, is a violation of these premises.

"As a Christian and as a president who was severely provoked by international crises, I became thoroughly familiar with the principles of a just war, and it is clear that a substantially unilateral attack on Iraq does not meet these standards. This is an almost universal conviction of religious leaders, with the most notable exception of a few spokesmen of the Southern Baptist Convention who are greatly influenced by their commitment to Israel based on eschatological (final days) theology.

"The preeminent criterion for a just war is that it can only be waged as a last resort, with all non-violent options exhausted. It is obvious that clear alternatives do exist, as previously proposed by our own leaders and approved by the United Nations. But now, with our own national security not directly threatened and despite the overwhelming opposition of most people and governments in the world, the United States seems deter-

mined to carry out military and diplomatic action that is almost unprecedented in the history of civilized nations. The first stage of our widely publicized war plan is to launch 3,000 bombs and missiles on a relatively defenseless Iraqi population within the first few hours of an invasion, with the purpose of so damaging and demoralizing the people that they will change their obnoxious leader, who will most likely be hidden and safe during the massive bombardment.

"Weapons used in war must discriminate between combatants and noncombatants. Extensive aerial bombardment, even with precise accuracy, always results in great 'collateral damage.' The American field commander, General Franks, is complaining in advance about many of the military targets being near hospitals, schools, mosques, and private homes.

"Violence used in the war must be proportional to the injury suffered. Despite Saddam Hussein's other serious crimes, American efforts to tie Iraq to the 9/11 terrorist attacks have been unconvincing.

"The attackers must have legitimate authority sanctioned by the society they profess to represent. The unanimous vote of approval in the Security Council

to eliminate Iraq's weapons of mass destruction can still be honored, but our announced goals are now to achieve regime change and to establish a Pax Americana in the region, perhaps occupying the ethnically divided country for as long as a decade. For these objectives, we do not have international authority. Other members of the UN Security Council have so far resisted the enormous economic and political influence that is being exerted from Washington, and we are faced with the possibility of either a failure to get the necessary votes or else a veto from Russia, France, or China. Although Turkey may still be enticed by enormous financial rewards and partial future control of the Kurds and oil in Northern Iraq, its democratic parliament has at least added its voice to the worldwide expressions of concern.

"The peace to be established must be a clear improvement over what exists. Although there are visions of a panacea of peace and democracy in Iraq, it is quite possible that the aftermath of a successful military invasion will destabilize the region, and that aroused terrorists might detract from the personal safety of our people and the security of our nation.

Also, to defy overwhelming world opposition will threaten a deep and permanent fracture of the United Nations as a viable institution for world peace.

". . . the heartfelt sympathy and friendship offered to us after the 9/11 terrorist attacks, even from formerly antagonistic regimes, has been largely dissipated, and increasingly unilateral and domineering policies have brought our country to its lowest level of international distrust and antagonism in memory. We will surely decline further in stature if we launch a war in clear defiance of UN opposition, but to continue using the presence and threat of our military power to force Iraq's compliance with all UN resolutions — with war as a final option — will enhance our status as a champion of peace and justice."

Despite this tragically prescient prewar statement and others like it, the United States rejected international restraints against the use of force and invaded Iraq with overwhelming military power. There was never any doubt about the outcome of this conflict, since for more than a decade there had been tight international limitations on Iraq's acquisition of advanced weaponry, and for every three dollars in America's military budget, the Iraqis were spending only one cent. The tragic misjudgment was that our brave military forces were going into what was pictured to be a warm welcome by liberated Iraqis. Instead, we have suffered at least fifteen thousand casualties, including more than seventeen hundred killed, 93 percent of them since Baghdad fell.

The average number of American military fatalities was forty-eight per month before Saddam Hussein was captured; it then increased to seventy-eight per month. Strangely, the U.S. news media seem insensitive to the casualties. The ombudsman of the *Washington Post* acknowledged, for instance, "Between April 1 and June 23, as I write this, 193 U.S. service members died in Iraq, and there wasn't a single, major front-page headline that captured this as it was unfolding or summed things up at any point."

One of the strangest of our government's decisions has been to restrict awareness of American casualties. Rarely are the wounded mentioned or visited by our leaders, and everything possible is done to prevent any public notice of the caskets returning to the stateside mortuary at Dover Air Force Base in Delaware. Lawsuits have been filed on behalf of mothers and wives who have been denied permission to meet the bodies of their dead family members at Dover or at other military bases.

We and our British allies have made an official decision to refrain from counting or estimating the number of civilian deaths, and there are wide ranges in the published numbers. A respected British medical journal, *Lancet*, has reported that allied forces (especially the air force) have killed a hundred thousand Iraqi noncombatants. The only estimates from official American sources are about twenty-four thousand, limited just to those reported in the Western news media. The actual figures are somewhere between these extremes.

In addition to Iraqis killed during American military operations, Iraqi civilians and police officers died at a rate of more than 800 a month between August 2004 and May 2005, according to figures released in June 2005 by Iraq's interior ministry, with the death rate increasing after the January election.

Regardless of the exact number of casualties, there are two basic facts to be remembered: the war was unjust and unnecessary, and our armed forces in Iraq deserve extraordinary gratitude and admiration for their special courage and effectiveness. The fact is that, unlike during other times of national threat or crisis, <u>the United States of America is not at war.</u> To an extraordinary degree, the entire burden of the conflict has been focused just on a few military personnel and their families, with no financial sacrifice or discomfort among 99.5 percent of the American people. Five hundred thousand troops were involved in the first Gulf War in the limited goal of evicting Iraq from Kuwait, but this time only one-third as many have been repeatedly sent to conquer and hold a large and complex nation.

The survivors are receiving their well-deserved praise, but our family went through a different kind of conflict when our oldest son left college to volunteer for service in Vietnam. That was an extremely unpopular American adventure. I remember that when Jack was on military leave for brief periods, he was ridiculed by his peers and former classmates for being gullible and naïve, and preferred not to wear his uniform. It was several years after the Vietnam War ended before these brave young men were finally honored as heroes.

A basic question to be asked is, "Has the Iraqi war reduced the threat of terrorism?"

Unfortunately, the answer is "No." Not only have we lost the almost unanimous sympathy and support that was offered to us throughout the world after the attack of 9/11, but there is direct evidence that the Iraqi war has actually increased the terrorist threat. In testimony before the Congress, CIA Director Porter Goss stated, "Islamic extremists are exploiting the Iraqi conflict to recruit new anti-U.S. jihadists [holy warriors]. . . . These jihadists who survive will leave Iraq experienced and focus on acts of urban terrorism." He added that the war "has become a cause for extremists."

To corroborate his opinion, the U.S. National Counter-terrorism Center reported that the number of serious international terrorist incidents more than tripled in 2004. "Significant" attacks grew to more than 650, up from the previous record of about 175 in 2003. Terrorist incidents in Iraq also dramatically increased, from 22 attacks to 198, or nine times the previous year's total — after the U.S. handover of political authority to an interim Iraqi government. It is obvious that the war has turned Iraq into the world's most effective terrorist training camp, perhaps more dangerous than Afghanistan under the

Taliban. Also, instead of our being able to use Iraq as a permanent base from which to pressure Iran and Syria, there seems to be a growing allegiance between the evolving Iraqi government and its fundamentalist Shiite neighbors, which may greatly strengthen Iran's strategic position in the Middle East.

The adoption of preemptive war as an American policy has forced the United States to renounce existing treaties and alliances as unnecessary constraints on our superpower's freedom to act unilaterally. Another serious consequence of this policy is the likelihood that other aggressive nations will adopt the same policy of attacking to remove leaders they consider to be undesirable.

When the United States orchestrated the first step toward potential democracy in Iraq early in 2005, there was a dramatic demonstration of courage and commitment to freedom as a large number of Shiite Muslims and Kurds went to the polls in the face of intimidation from Sunni dissidents and terrorist groups. The next steps toward writing a constitution and then forming a representative government are still not predictable as I write this text, but there is great concern about whether Sunnis will cooperate and how dominant the religious laws will be. The ruling Shiite religious parties are demanding that provisions of the Koran, called Sharia, become the supreme authority on marriage, divorce, and inheritance issues. It would be ironic if crucial women's rights that survived Saddam Hussein's regime were lost under the new "democratic" government sponsored and protected by the United States.

It will be a notable achievement if success can be realized, and despite the uncertainties and an increase in the fervor of terrorists, this effort to bring democracy to Iraq deserves the world's support.

There is no doubt that America must accomplish its fundamental objectives before withdrawing our troops from Iraq, but those goals have never been clearly delineated. It is likely that political pressures from a disillusioned American public will be a major factor in setting the minimal goals and time schedule for U.S. troop withdrawal. We should provide the people with water, sewage, communications, electricity, and the ability to produce and market their oil. The Iraqis must have a security force as effective as the one we dismantled, to support a stable and democratic government.

A basic question that will determine the final outcome is whether American leaders will insist on permanent military bases and dominant economic involvement in the country, or make it clear that we have no plans to maintain a continuing presence for our own benefit.

To a surprising and disturbing degree, most Arabs in the region do not agree with my favorable assessment of the democratic effort. In a respected survey done by Zogby International in Egypt, Saudi Arabia, Morocco, Jordan, Lebanon, and the United Arab Emirates and reported in March 2005, an overwhelming majority of Arabs did not believe that U.S. policy in Iraq was motivated by the spread of democracy in the region, and believed that the Middle East had become less democratic after the Iraq war and that Iraqis were worse off than they had been before the conflict. Overall approval ratings of the United States were at an unprecedented low of 2 percent in Egypt, 4 percent in Saudi Arabia, 11 percent in Morocco, 14 percent in the United Arab Emirates, 15 percent in Jordan, with a high of only 20 percent in Lebanon.

These were the Arab countries that had

the closest historical ties with America. More than three-fourths of the Arab respondents professed support for democratic principles of government, but they strongly condemned the attack on Iraq and the apparent bias of the United States against the rights of the Palestinians. Despite our admirable democratic efforts, these are not good omens for our policies in the region.

As I have described earlier, one of the characteristics of fundamentalists is to forgo discussion or negotiation to resolve differences, interpreting this as a sign of weakness in adhering to their own principles. The most telltale distinction between Republicans and Democrats is their preference between ways of resolving controversial international issues — reliance on force, or diplomacy.

Our nation is clearly divided on the basic response to the international challenges that confront us. It is almost universally assumed that the American homeland will never be completely secure. There will be a lasting threat of terrorism, most likely from relatively weak organizations that could not hope to challenge any aspect of our overwhelming military strength.

What are our best responses? Is it better

to cherish our historic role as the great champion of human rights, or to abandon our high domestic and international standards in response to threats? Is it better to set a firm example of reducing reliance on nuclear weapons and their further proliferation, or to insist on our right (and that of others) to retain our arsenals, expand them, and therefore abrogate or derogate control agreements negotiated for many decades? Are we best served by espousing peace as a national priority unless our security is directly threatened, or by proclaiming an unabridged right to attack other nations unilaterally to change an unsavory regime or for other purposes? Is a declaration of "You are either with us or against us" superior to forming alliances based on a clear comprehension of mutual interests? When there are serious differences with other nations, is it best to permit direct negotiations to resolve the problems, or to brand those who differ as international pariahs — and to refuse to permit such discussions?

Most of these questions are already being answered by our government's policies — policies that are predicated on the basic premises of fundamentalism. It is not yet clear if the American people approve.

15

WHERE ARE THE MAJOR THREATS TO THE ENVIRONMENT?

One of the most prevailing bipartisan commitments during the past 150 years has been America's enhancement and protection of the environment. This has included the formation, protection, and expansion of our national parks and wilderness areas; the initiation and strengthening of laws to ensure the purity of air and water; and efforts to protect citizens in all countries from the threats of pollution and toxic wastes. The first national park, Yellowstone, was established during the administration of Ulysses S. Grant. Theodore Roosevelt and his successors expanded the system, and Richard Nixon signed legislation setting high purity standards for air and water.

When statehood came to Alaska, President Dwight Eisenhower realized that there were vast areas of land that needed to be allocated among the state and federal governments, Eskimos and other Native Americans, and some private interests. The House of Representatives was able to address one especially sensitive issue, with legislation recommending that 9 million acres of pristine land along the northern shore of Alaska be protected permanently from any commercial development. When the two Alaska senators blocked Senate action, President Eisenhower accomplished his goal by establishing the Arctic National Wildlife Range "for the purpose of preserving unique wildlife, wilderness and recreational values." The status of other vast territories in Alaska was left unsettled.

This was the situation I inherited twenty-one years later. Resolving the complex and controversial questions concerning land distribution required four full years of work by my administration and a bipartisan coalition in the Congress, but we finally forged the Alaska National Interest Lands Conservation Act (ANILCA), which allocated all the available territory. In doing so, we were able to double the size of our nation's park system and triple our wilderness areas.

The House-passed bill included my priority recommendation protecting the Eisenhower area — including *every acre* of the present Arctic National Wildlife Refuge — but once again the last-minute opposition of Alaska's senators, heavily influenced by the oil industry, blocked the inclusion of full wilderness status for the refuge. We were successful in including a requirement that a completely new act of Congress be passed if the area should ever be opened to oil drilling. Our natural presumption was that it would be virtually impossible for both houses of Congress and any president all to agree to despoil the area.

That expectation was realized during the next twenty-five years, based on two fundamental premises: First, the refuge is an undisturbed habitat of obvious, manifold, and world-class wildlife and wilderness values. This is exactly the same reason that we protect Yellowstone and Yosemite. Second, enlightened American political leaders have known that our nation's energy future rests not on wrecking pristine natural environments but on far more cost-effective efficiency alternatives that will give us more certain and permanent independence from foreign oil.

This precious area is the ecological heart of a refuge that links to millions of additional acres of protected wildlife habitat in the northwest corner of Canada. The pageant of wildlife that flourishes here in its wilderness home is North America's Serengeti, and has fired the innate love of our people for their natural heritage.

Rosalynn and I have been fortunate enough to kneel on the tundra of this coastal plain as tens of thousands of caribou passed around us in their timeless migration to vital calving and nursery grounds — the very area now targeted for oil development. We have watched a herd of musk oxen circle around their young to protect them — but we knew that their defensive behavior could not protect them from industrial development. The same is true of the polar bear and the millions of migratory waterfowl that nest on this coastal tundra. This is their wilderness home.

The oil industry finally seemed to prevail in March 2005, when a single political party controlled the White House and both houses of Congress, and a legislative maneuver was used to attach the destructive provision to a budget bill that was impervious to the opposition of senators attempting to protect the refuge. Even if this legislation is finally approved, there is still some hope that responsible oil companies will not betray the American people by drilling. As a consumer of petroleum products, I would make my last choice for a supplier any of those oil companies who were drilling in our refuge, and there may be several million other environmentalists with the same inclination.

Our nation consumes 7 billion barrels of oil per year, and even if the refuge provided the hoped-for 1 million barrels per day, the slight annual increase in domestic supply would not significantly lessen our dependence on foreign oil. At best, according to various energy experts, the refuge would yield less than a year's supply of oil for the United States.

To become less dependent on foreign oil is a worthy objective, but there are permanent and far more effective ways to achieve this goal. The average efficiency of American automobiles was only 12 miles per gallon when I became president, and I worked with automobile manufacturers and the Congress to implement a commitment to increase efficiency, in prescribed steps, to 27.5 miles per gallon. Since I left office, these requirements have been periodically lowered, through carefully crafted loopholes, and efficiencies have dropped again.

Motor vehicles now use 40 percent of our nation's oil, and the average engine horsepower of trucks and SUVs has doubled since 1980, with their weight increasing by almost 1,000 pounds. Large SUVs and Hummers that weigh twice this much are exempt from efficiency regulations.

The tragedy of the decision to savage the Alaska refuge is that when oil from the area might reach peak production, fifteen to twenty years from now, it will equal the amount that could be saved by requiring the efficiency of "light trucks" (SUVs) to be the same as that of ordinary cars (20 miles per gallon). To reach the target we set in 1980 would result in far more savings. Perhaps not surprisingly, political pressures from the oil industry and automobile manufacturers have prevailed on this issue, and gas guzzlers have become a major product in our country. This foolish government decision against fuel economy might be a serious long-term blow to the American automobile industry in its competition with more efficient vehicles manufactured in Japan and Europe as fuel prices inevitably rise in the future.

Another sad need in our country is the routine maintenance of our national parks. Since the Alaska lands bill was enacted a quarter century ago, Congress has added more than 80 parks to the system, for a total of 388, but neither presidents nor members of Congress have provided adequate funds for their upkeep. Governor George W. Bush made this the central issue of his environmental agenda during the 2000 presidential campaign, chastising his predecessors for allowing the parks to decay. He pledged to spend $1 billion a year in new money over five years to meet the long-overdue needs for upkeep, then estimated to be $4.9 billion. Only 18 percent of this amount has been forthcoming, and in 2005 the nonpartisan Congressional Research Service estimated the backlog at $7.5 billion. The failure to correct this mistake is obviously bipartisan.

Almost simultaneously with the passage of ANILCA in 1980 came the completion of work on what was known as Superfund legislation. I had long been concerned about the emission of toxic materials by some irresponsible corporations, and working with a bipartisan Congress we established legal requirements that such wastes be reduced drastically and that those responsible be required to finance the cleanup of their poisonous deposits. Also, a small surcharge on polluting chemical companies established a permanent fund to cover future costs. Now, with the advent of a new administration in Washington, industry lobbyists have been able to prevail again, as the "polluters pay" principle was abandoned. American taxpayers were forced to pay about 80 percent of the cleanup costs in 2004 and will bear the total bill in fiscal year 2005. There is little financial incentive for unscrupulous corporations to restrict their dumping of toxic wastes.

One of the most controversial and universally condemned decisions made in recent years by top American leaders was to reject participation in the laboriously negotiated international agreement to control greenhouse gases, which are causing an increase in the planet's temperature. It has become widely known that man-made gases, mostly oxides, rise into the stratosphere and create a blanket similar to the plastic or glass bubble that surrounds a greenhouse. The sun's rays enter, and an increasing amount of heat is retained instead of being dissipated from the earth's atmosphere.

So far as I know, this issue first came under serious discussion while I was president, when scientists in the National Oceanic and Atmospheric Administration and the National Academy of Sciences began to express concern about the adverse effects of carbon dioxide building up in the atmosphere. The problem was so serious that my science adviser, Dr. Frank Press, asked the National Academy to study the issue, and a distinguished panel was convened at the Woods Hole Research Center in Massachusetts in the summer of 1979. The scientists concluded that the planet's temperature would increase about five degrees Fahrenheit when the carbon dioxide level doubled. The official report to me added, "We have tried but have been unable to find any overlooked or underestimated physical effects that could reduce the warming."

The scientists' warnings are coming true. There is now a massive melting of mountain glaciers and ice in the polar regions, the level of the seas is rising, and marked abnormalities are observed in the behavior and survivability of sensitive species. This is happening quite rapidly, and it is expected, for instance, that all the ancient ice formations in Glacier National Park will completely vanish by 2030. Rosalynn and I were in Alaska recently to celebrate the twenty-fifth anniversary of ANILCA and were greeted by headlines about the potential extinction of polar bears, along with articles about the inundation of Eskimo villages due to the loss of ice shields and the rise of sea levels. We visited one of the glaciers in the Kenai Fjords region, which was rapidly melting away.

Both President George H. W. Bush and President Bill Clinton helped to negotiate the Kyoto Protocol, designed to establish a worldwide commitment to control atmospheric pollution and reduce the buildup of gases that are the cause of global warming. The history of this effort is another disturbing indication of the recent change in our nation's values. By 1988, the international community had become deeply concerned about the problem, and an international panel on climate change was formed. After two years of intense scientific analysis, a report was issued stating that the planet was warming and that human activity was causing it.

In 1992, the largest group of world leaders in history met in Rio de Janeiro, Brazil, in what became known as the Earth Summit. U.S. President George H. W. Bush and others called on the world to stabilize greenhouse gas emissions by 2000 at the 1990 level, especially carbon dioxide.

The United States and other nations ratified this convention, with the treaty legally binding on the nations involved. Importantly, President Bush negotiated an agreement to allow developing nations to be excluded from the restrictions, since industrialized countries are the overwhelming contributors to the troubling emissions. It was further agreed that parties to the treaty would meet annually to assess further scientific knowledge about the causes and seriousness of global warming.

After five years of additional study, a second report was issued that confirmed that "the balance of evidence pointed to a discernable human influence on the global climate system" and added that "climate change represented a danger to humanity." This serious finding led to a 1997 conference of the participating nations in Kyoto, Japan, where a commitment was made to reduce the 1990 level of greenhouse gas emissions overall by 5 percent between 2008 and 2012. Each country signing this protocol determined its own voluntary reduction, with Germany's commitment at 25 percent, the United Kingdom's 15 percent, and the United States pledging a more modest reduction of 7 percent.

As national leaders continued their intense study and negotiation, newly inaugurated President George W. Bush announced that the Kyoto agreement's mandatory reductions in greenhouse gases and short timetable would be too expensive and unwise when the United States was facing energy problems. He agreed, however, to continue working with other leaders in preparation for a long-scheduled international conference in Bonn, Germany. There, the world powers reached a historic agreement just before dawn on July 29, 2001, but the new American leader reiterated his rejection of all our nation's previous commitments. One hundred eighty countries (that is, the whole world except for the United States and one other) agreed to the rules for implementing the Kyoto Protocol. Despite American opposition, a proviso was adopted that it go into effect when officially adopted by countries that, collectively, were responsible for 55 percent of the global greenhouse emissions. This milestone was reached when Russia ratified the agreement, and after ninety days, the Kyoto Protocol became international law, on February 16, 2005.

In April 2005, a definitive report was published in the journal *Science* by a group of scientists led by James E. Hansen, a NASA climatologist, that should dispel all doubts about forecasts of climate change. After a five-year study using more than two thousand monitoring stations around the globe, they determined that temperatures would continue a slow rise even if greenhouse gases are capped immediately, and will "spin out of control" if strong corrective action is not taken. An increase of ten degrees Fahrenheit this century could occur. Based on additional scientific proof of the long-range problem, Holland has committed to cut emissions by 80 percent, the United Kingdom by 60 percent, and Germany by 50 percent in the next forty years.

Our government leaders' insistence on their continuing right to avoid emission restraints has become one of the most prevalent rallying points of people around the world who condemn the United States and its rejection of environmental standards. Robert May, one of Great Britain's chief scientists and president of the Royal Society, said the Bush administration is resisting "scientific fact" and is trying to superimpose "one fundamentalist ideology on the rest of the G-8."

This pattern of carelessness or disregard

also applies to America's own environment. Under original provisions, landmark legislation dealing with clean air and water, mining, grazing, forestry, toxic wastes, and the protection of endangered species has been reauthorized regularly, with higher standards expected to be imposed at each step as technology improved. With antienvironmentalist Republicans dominating the key congressional committees, all of the relevant laws are long overdue for reauthorization and there is little apparent enthusiasm from the White House or any other source to address these issues.

Instead of increasing standards, recent proposals from the administration would allow older, coal-burning power plants to avoid installing pollution controls when they repair or modernize, would permit violations of health standards concerning soot and smog to continue until 2015 or longer, and would allow twice as much sulfur dioxide and one and a half times as much nitrogen oxide for a decade longer than would the existing Clean Air Act. One Republican congressional proposal would allow communities whose air pollution comes from hundreds of miles away to delay meeting national air quality standards for ten years, or until their upwind neighbors clean up their own air. Strongly supported by polluting industries, this law could create an unending blame game and be another serious setback to the Clean Air Act.

This abandonment of many elements crucial for preserving environmental quality has been a prevailing pattern during the past four years.

There are strong and often evenly divided partisan debates on some major issues, but this is not the case in protecting the quality of our environment. Some prominent Republicans are deeply worried about their party leaders' lack of concern about global warming and other issues. When asked about the policies of the president and some congressional colleagues, Senator John McCain said, "There's no justification for not taking action now, but we have a tough task ahead in convincing the administration. The White House stance on climate change is terribly disappointing. Unfortunately, the special interests rule in Washington, D.C. The major lobbies, including the utilities, wield enormous power on Capitol Hill." He added, "Are we going to hand our children and grandchildren a world vastly different from the one that we now inhabit?" Led by

Republicans, the U.S. Senate resisted intense opposition from the White House and passed a non-binding resolution in June 2005 favoring a program of mandatory control of the emission of gases that contribute to global warming.

As with American automobile manufacturers, our country's major industries dealing with energy production and environmental equipment will be at a great disadvantage in worldwide markets if they do not accommodate these restraints on global warming. In fact, General Electric and others have already announced plans to support compliance with the Kyoto treaty provisions. Despite U.S. government opposition, clean technology is the wave of the future.

Overwhelmingly, opinion polls reveal that Americans support provisions that preserve air and water quality, control pollution, protect wildlife, and expand and preserve parklands. These firm convictions hold even when the question includes specific tax increases required for funding. In public referenda of this kind in forty-three states during the past ten years, 1,065 out of 1,376 conservation measures have been approved by voters.

There are geopolitical consequences of

our government's new policies, as we continue to reward nondemocratic oil-rich foreign nations and retain our dependence on them, build up the greenhouse effect with factory and automobile exhausts, and face an inevitable political and economic competition with China and other rapidly developing countries as they assuage their skyrocketing thirst for oil from the same sources. About 800 million automobiles now operate in the world, and it is estimated that with economic development in China and India this number will increase, year by year, to 3.25 billion cars within the next forty years. It is sobering to visualize this escalating impact on the planet's environment.

A much higher fuel efficiency for power plants and for vehicles is by far the best response to this situation, along with the use of other sources of energy for electric power plants. Nuclear fuel is a promising, though limited, alternative. About 20 percent of U.S. electricity now comes from the 103 nuclear reactors in operation, and this could be increased. Technological advances have dramatically improved safety, and the problem of nuclear waste products can be reduced. Recently I attended the commissioning of a submarine that bears my name — fifty years after I helped with the development of the first nuclear ships. At that time, the reactor cores had to be replaced within three years, but fuel rods in the new submarine will last for at least thirty-five years, or the entire life of the ship.

America is by far the world's leading polluter, and our government's abandonment of its responsibilities is just another tragic step in a series of actions that have departed from the historic bipartisan protection of the global environment. Our proper stewardship of God's world is a personal and political moral commitment.

16

THE WORLD'S GREATEST CHALLENGE IN THE NEW MILLENNIUM

There is an overwhelming religious mandate, often ignored by fundamentalists, to alleviate the plight of those who are in need. Jim Wallis, editor of *Sojourners* magazine, reports that he and a group of other seminary students searched the Bible to find every verse that referred to wealth and poverty. They were impressed to discover that one out of sixteen verses in the New Testament, one in ten in three of the Gospels, and one in seven in the Gospel of Luke referred to money or to the poor. In the Hebrew Scriptures, only idolatry was mentioned more times than the relationship between rich and poor.

When we recite the Lord's Prayer and pray for God's kingdom to come on earth, we are asking for an end to political and economic injustice within worldly regimes.

In fact, all major religious faiths are shaped by prophetic mandates to do justice, love mercy, protect and care for widows and orphans, and exemplify God's compassion for the poor and victimized. It is clear that proper treatment of the poor should be an extremely high priority among those who shape American policies. In fact, this criterion may be the most amenable to exact measurement, so that direct comparisons can be made among those who profess to espouse the basic moral values of our nation.

As the year 2000 approached, I was invited to speak at a major forum and asked to address this question: "What is the world's greatest challenge in the new millennium?" It was an interesting assignment, and I replied, with little doubt, that the greatest challenge we face is the growing chasm between the rich and poor people on earth. There is not only a great disparity between the two, but the gap is steadily widening. At the beginning of the last century, the ten richest countries were nine times wealthier than the ten poorest ones. In 1960 the ratio was 30:1. At the beginning of this century, average income per person in the twenty richest nations was $27,591 and in the poorest nations only $211, a ratio of 131:1!

It is a source of pride that the average family in the United States has an income of about $55,000 a year, but we must remember that more than half the world's people live on less than $2 a day, and 1.2 billion people have to survive on half that amount. Imagine for a moment that we have only $1 a day — for food, housing, and clothing. There would obviously be nothing left for health care or education, and it would be difficult to retain our self-respect or hope for a brighter future.

Almost all of my American readers and my own family are among those with adequate incomes, but all too few of us are acquainted with the poor. During the past two decades, my wife and I have represented The Carter Center in visits to more than 120 nations in order to know who their people are and how best to meet some of their needs. We now have programs in 65 nations, and not surprisingly, 35 of them are in sub-Saharan Africa. We always remember that in the Universal Declaration of Human Rights, one of the guarantees for all persons is a standard of living adequate for the health and well-being of themselves and their families.

In my speech at the beginning of the new

millennium, I outlined a few proposals for meeting this standard, including increased development assistance with fewer strings, forgiveness of foreign debts of the poorest nations, seeking peaceful solutions when there are known threats to peace, getting to know the poor, giving people authority and responsibility over their own affairs, enhancing cooperation among donors, and recognizing the inevitable impact of abject poverty on human rights, violence, and susceptibility to recruitment for violent acts.

Our Center's programs have shown that with wise use of even limited resources, extremely poor people demonstrate remarkable intelligence, innovation, and effectiveness. There are only 150 people who work at The Carter Center — they include landscapers and receptionists, as well as experts deployed to African villages — so we have to rely on other people to magnify the effectiveness of our work. For most projects, I negotiate a contract in advance with a nation's top leaders, usually agreeing that we will provide only one foreign expert. Local citizens, whom we train, must perform the necessary tasks and be paid by their own government. We have found them to be very dedicated and competent.

In teaching African farmers to produce more food grain (primarily corn, rice, wheat, sorghum, or millet), our usual level of participation in each country during the past twenty growing seasons has been limited to about sixty thousand families. Often at an annual cost of no more than $10 per family, they are introduced to the best available seed for their altitude and latitude and taught how to plant in contour rows, to control weeds, to harvest at the best time, to store the gathered crop, and to use enough fertilizer to maintain soil fertility. Still using simple hand tools and manual labor, they are able to double or triple their production.

We also decided to help eradicate a crippling disease called Guinea worm (dracunculiasis), which has afflicted people throughout recorded history. Depending on drinking water from ponds that fill during the rainy season, villagers imbibe worm eggs that grow in the stagnant water. After a year, the egg grows within the body into a worm about thirty inches in length, which then stings the inside of the skin, forming a large sore that destroys muscle tissue and incapacitates the sufferer with intense pain. Taking about a month to emerge, the worm lays countless eggs as the victim wades into the pond for more water or to ease the pain.

Rosalynn and I first saw the ravages of Guinea worm in small and isolated villages in Ghana, where two-thirds of the people had worms emerging from their bodies. Some could not drag themselves from their huts to the village commons to greet us. My most unforgettable case was a beautiful young woman who had a worm emerging from the nipple of her breast and who was later discovered to have eleven other worms coming from different places in her body.

We found 3.5 million cases of the disease in 23,700 villages in India, Pakistan, Yemen, and eighteen countries across sub-Saharan Africa, and began the slow and methodical task of instructing people in every affected village on the necessary steps to protect themselves. They could filter every drink (through special cloth contributed by DuPont), eliminate the eggs from their pond with a pesticide, or secure water from a deep well. If every villager did this for a year and infected people stayed out of the water, the pond would no longer receive new eggs and harbor the disease, and the cycle would be permanently broken. The result of the people's commitment has been spectacular, so that there are now less than one half of 1 percent as many cases, and we are able to focus on the remaining ones in just a few infected villages.

To prevent the loss of sight from river blindness (onchocerciasis), The Carter Center treated more than 10 million people in Africa and Latin America during 2004 with a free medicine furnished to us by Merck & Co. Although the problem in Africa is much more deeply entrenched and persistent, and repeated annual doses are required, we have found that two treatments each year to more than 85 percent of the population in infected areas will eliminate the disease entirely in this hemisphere. This is a goal we expect to reach by 2007.

Among other ongoing health projects of The Carter Center, the control of trachoma is especially interesting. This disease is an infection caused by filthy eyes and is the number one cause of preventable blindness. From a distance, we first thought that children in a Masai or Dinka village were wearing glasses, but on approaching them we realized that there were rings of black flies almost permanently surrounding their eyes to obtain moisture. Infected with trachoma, the upper eyelid turns inward so that the lashes slash the cornea as the eye blinks, causing blindness. I knew of a few cases of this disease when I was a child in southwest Georgia, when very few of our poorest neighbors were blessed with an outdoor toilet like the one in our backyard, and flies were prevalent.

We provide an antibiotic tablet (furnished by Pfizer Inc.), instruction on washing the face and how to perform simple surgery on the eyelid, and advice about village sanitation to reduce the cloud of flies. The normal custom was for humans to urinate and defecate on the ground around their homes, as was done in other parts of the world in bygone years. Just three years ago, we began to teach villagers how to dig a hole in the ground, put a mud brick or concrete ring around it, and erect some kind of screen.

We have been amazed at the response of people to these new latrines, especially in Ethiopia, and to learn that the primary thrust for building them has come from women. The reason is that men have customarily relieved themselves openly at any time of the day, but it has been taboo for women to have the same privilege except at night. Women's liberation has now come to life, and 89,500 latrines have already been constructed in one region of Ethiopia during this brief period of time!

The purpose of these accounts is to emphasize the profound human needs that exist among the poorest of people and their enthusiastic and effective responses when they are given a modest chance (by the rich) to improve their lives.

Our entire society is becoming increasingly divided, not necessarily between black, white, or Hispanic, but primarily between the rich and the poor. Many of us don't even know a poor person. If we have a maid or yardman, we would probably not go to their house and have a cup of coffee in their kitchen or know the names of their teenage sons — or, God forbid, invite them to come to our house or to take their children to a baseball game with our kids. Even those of us who accept an all-inclusive Christ as Savior are strongly inclined to live separate lives and avoid forming cohesive personal relations with our neighbors. Rosalynn and I have been equally susceptible to this failing.

One of the most natural ways to reach out to needy people has been through Habitat for Humanity, with its international headquarters just ten miles from our home. This has become a surprisingly well-known aspect of our post–White House years, although we just send out some fund-raising letters and lead a group of volunteers for one week each year to build homes somewhere in the world. We have done this for more than twenty years in ghetto areas, rural towns, and a Native American reservation in the United States, and also in Mexico, Canada, Korea, the Philippines, Hungary, and South Africa. We plan to build homes in India in 2006.

We work side by side with poor families who will be able to own the houses because Habitat follows the biblical prohibition against charging interest. This has been an enjoyable and heartwarming opportunity for us and many others to put our religious faith into practice, and it demonstrates vividly the importance and difficulty of reaching out to needy people.

I always remember a cartoon in one of the Habitat newspapers. It was a panorama of a village, maybe from an airplane flying overhead. Some people are playing tennis, some are riding bicycles, others are in automobiles, or teaching school, maybe some plowing with tractors, and all have little bubbles above their heads, with the words "What can just one person do?" When combined, the small individual contributors of caring, friendship, forgiveness, and love, each of us different from our next-door neighbors, can form a phalanx, an army, with great capability.

Despite all the goodwill and generosity that exist among American citizens, the amount of foreign assistance going from our government to the poor is still embarrassingly small. Predictably, much of the U.S. government's foreign aid goes to friendly nations and military allies, and Washington restricts many other kinds of assistance with all kinds of political strings. It is distressing to see our great nation defaulting on its obligation to share a respectable portion of our wealth with the most destitute people on earth.

Since the end of the Cold War, when the United States and the Soviet Union were competing to give assistance to the world's poorest nations to induce them to come within our respective political and military orbits, insensitivity to these humanitarian needs has been a bipartisan failure.

In March 2002 I represented The Carter Center at an international conference in Monterrey, Mexico, convened by the United Nations to address the related problems of extreme poverty and child mortality. A great number of top political leaders participated in person, including the U.S. president, and they pledged a large increase in funds to meet this "millennium challenge." Many of us were thrilled by these commitments, but there is now a prevailing sense of disillusionment with America's performance.

Sharing wealth with those that are starving and suffering unnecessarily is a value by which a nation's moral values are measured, and there is a strange and somewhat disturbing situation in our country. Americans are willing to be generous in helping others — and they believe that our government gives as much as 15 percent of our federal budget in foreign aid. But we are, in fact, the stingiest of all industrialized nations. We allot about one-thirtieth as much as is commonly believed. Our gross national income (GNI) is about $11 trillion, of which we share with poor nations only *sixteen cents* out of each $100. If we add all the donations from American foundations and from other private sources to the government's funds, the total still amounts to just *twenty-two cents* per $100 of national income.

When confronted with these embarrassing facts, many well-informed Americans reply that we are quite generous in responding to catastrophes, such as the recent tsunami damage in Asia. This is true, and an admirable characteristic of our citizens, but most people do not realize that dealing with persistent suffering is equally important. There were about 200,000 fatalities in the eleven nations struck by the tidal wave, but 165,000 die of malaria, 140,000 of diarrhea, and 240,000 of AIDS *every month!* About $2.50 a year from each American and European citizen could mount an effective global fight against malaria.

Even these disturbingly low figures about foreign aid are misleading, because they include special help for "strategic" countries (many of which are middle-income but considered to be valuable political partners), and a good portion of our foreign aid is in surplus grain that cannot be sold in the United States. (About half of these food grain costs are for transportation.) Even the trickle of money that remains for such programs as education, health, housing, or sanitation rarely goes to the local people themselves, but mostly goes to American consultants who station themselves in the needy nations.

President Bush announced in June 2005 a plan to furnish $1.2 billion for a five-year campaign against malaria in fifteen African countries where 175 million people are at risk. This would be a major contribution — if the promise is fulfilled. The claims of generosity are quite popular both at home and abroad, but most previous commitments have been abandoned by the White House, slashed by the Congress, or so bogged down in administrative complexities that little support actually reaches the people in need.

Soon after the 2002 Monterrey Conference, President George W. Bush announced a Millennium Challenge fund of $5 billion annually for development aid, but three years later only $400,000 (less than 1 percent) has actually been distributed. Another example is Washington's official announcement of one of its most noteworthy achievements: that more than forty-one thousand AIDS victims in Botswana have received life-extending treatments from the United States. Top managers of Botswana's treatment program were irate, reporting that no American money had arrived and calling the U.S. claims "false, and a gross misrepresentation of the facts." The more accurate number of patients in Botswana who had been put on treatment because of American help: zero.

The annual United States foreign aid budget for fighting malaria, for instance, has been $90 million, but 95 percent of the money is being spent on consultants and less than 5 percent on mosquito nets, drugs, and insecticide spraying to fight the disease. Senator Sam Brownback, a conservative Kansas Republican, has complained about this policy, and has introduced a bill to force the administration to spend half of its malaria budget on treatment. Brownback pointed out that the government's list of contractors on its Web site has not been updated for four years. The senator said he had received only "vague descriptions and math that doesn't add up," and demanded an audit by the government accountability office.

According to Jeffrey Sachs, director of the U.N. Millennium Project, which was established to implement the promises made in Monterrey, annual U.S. aid for sub-Saharan Africa was about $3 billion in 2003, of which "only $118 million was left for U.S. in-country operations and direct support for programs run by African governments and communities — just 18 cents for each of the nearly 650 million people in low-income nations — for investments in health, education, roads, power, water and sanitation, and democratic institutions in the region."

The Millennium Project has estimated that funds needed to fulfill commitments to needy people would amount to forty-four cents per $100 of gross national income in 2006 and increase to about seventy cents in 2015. To put this in perspective, just the *increase* in U.S. defense spending since 2001 has been $1.70 per $100 of GNI, while tax cuts (mostly for wealthy Americans) have amounted to $3.30 per $100 of GNI.

Always generous, Belgium, Sweden, the Netherlands, Luxembourg, Denmark, and Norway already exceed the 2015 figure, and Italy, France, Germany, and England have all agreed to meet the same target. Inevitably, our failure to meet responsibilities is becoming increasingly evident to people in other nations. These differences are likely to become more pronounced and perhaps even a source of criticism or condemnation in the years ahead, instead of portraying America as a powerful nation with strong moral values. More recently, our government has joined other nations in announcing the forgiveness of long-term debt, but will offset its share of this cost by cutting other aid. There is little doubt that with strong leadership from Washington, the people of our country would respond with greater generosity.

The sharply growing difference between our government's relative treatment of the rich and poor in our own country is much more apparent to American citizens. Our nation already has an extremely wide difference in income, and this disparity is growing rapidly. One indication of this gap is the ratio of incomes between the top and bottom one-fifths of a nation's population, which is four to one in Japan, seven to one in France, and eleven to one in the United States. Still, almost every decision made in Washington since 2000 has favored the wealthy, often at the expense of middle-class working families and the needy, and fundamental legislation on taxation and expenditures has been designed to perpetuate these trends. Assuming that security needs and existing entitlement programs will have to be funded, our unprecedented deficits mean that there will be fewer funds for maintaining — much less increasing — existing levels for health, education, welfare, housing, environmental quality, or the creation of jobs.

What has happened since 2000 is almost incredible. At that time, the Congressional Budget Office projected a surplus of $281 billion in 2001, to accumulate $5.6 trillion more within ten years. Instead, the federal deficit will be almost $400 billion in 2005, with spending maintained at about the same level but with extraordinary revenue reductions because of a series of massive tax cuts for wealthier Americans. Projections are that this level of deficit spending will continue. The national debt increased from $1 trillion to $4 trillion during the twelve years of the Reagan-Bush administrations, and since 2001 the Congress has had to increase the debt ceiling to $8 trillion, and it is heading in four more years to more than $10 trillion!

This fiscal approach, which will squeeze domestic programs, has been a well-understood goal of some conservative true believers since the origination of Social Security, Medicaid, Medicare, Head Start, and other humanitarian programs under Franklin Roosevelt, Harry Truman, and Lyndon Johnson. The inheritance tax was originated by Republican President Theodore Roosevelt, and is now an additional target for elimination — another massive reduction in the tax burden for the richest families in America.

The extraordinary deficits are not caused by spending increases at home or abroad. In 1962, federal spending amounted to just 19 percent of our economic output, and it had often been above 20 percent at different times. Now, even including the large expenditures for the Iraq war and homeland defense, expenditures are still only 20 percent. The problem is that recent tax cuts have reduced federal revenues to only 16 percent, by far the lowest level in modern history. The difference between these two figures indicates the magnitude of the deficit.

Under the tax cuts pushed through Congress since 2000, for every dollar in reductions for a middle-class family, the top 1 percent of households will receive $54, and those with $1 million or more in income will benefit by $191! During the first three years, the number of Americans living in poverty increased by 3.5 million, while the income for the four hundred wealthiest Americans jumped by 10 percent just in the year 2002. Another indication of the growing division between rich and poor in recent years is that the salaries of corporate chief executive officers have gone from forty times to four hundred times the average worker's pay. Even though there was strong growth in corporate profits, wages for the average worker fell in 2004, after adjusting for inflation — the first such drop in many years.

In addition to these radical changes within our domestic economy, our rapidly accumulating international debt has aroused serious concerns among independent financial experts. What Americans owe to foreigners is extremely high, and projected to double in four or five years. In March 2005, Warren Buffett's Berkshire Hathaway annual report stated: "The net ownership of the U.S. by other countries and their citizens a decade from now will amount to roughly $11 trillion [about equal to our current gross national income]. . . . A country that is now aspiring to an 'ownership society' will not find happiness in — and I'll use hyperbole here for emphasis — a 'sharecropper's society.' But that's precisely where our trade policies, supported by Republicans and Democrats alike, are taking us."

Compatible with overall economic philosophy, Wall Street's desire for investments of Social Security funds in the stock market became a major goal of top political leaders, but American citizens rejected a nationwide campaign by the president and — at least so far — have forced Congress to abandon this proposal.

To further enhance corporate privilege, the 2003 Medicare drug bill prohibits the

U.S. government from negotiating for lower drug prices, and pharmaceutical companies can continue to charge Americans much more than their customers in Canada and other nations. The Congressional Budget Office says that foreign drug prices range from 35 to 55 percent below U.S. levels. Not covered by this special provision, the Department of Veterans Affairs negotiates discounts of 50 percent or more. A responsible bill could have delivered almost twice as much coverage for the same price.

It is obvious that political contributions and effective lobbyists pay rich dividends, as has been vividly demonstrated by the tobacco industry. This is especially aggravating to me because my father, mother, both sisters, and only brother all died with cancer after becoming addicted to smoking cigarettes. Some progress has been made in recent years in requiring the manufacturers of this deadly product to compensate their victims and provide funding for health education (much of which has been used for other, nonrelated purposes). At the same time, tobacco companies have won the much more important battle by blocking any effective federal regulation of carcinogens in their highly publicized products.

Even tobacco firm executives were amazed in June 2005, when the highly political U.S. Justice Department scuttled the government's six-year effort to force the industry to finance a smoking-cessation effort. After spending more than $100 million on the lawsuit and producing expert evidence that $130 billion would be required over a twenty-five-year period, there was an abrupt announcement at the last minute that the demand would be reduced to just $10 billion during the next five years. The presiding federal judge expressed doubt about the political factors involved in this inexplicable sellout to the tobacco industry.

Despite touting concern for working Americans and private home ownership, key political leaders in Washington have successfully blocked any increase in the minimum wage, which has been held at only $5.15 per hour for eight years and not indexed to accommodate inflation. (In comparison, in U.S. dollars and based on currency values in April 2005, the minimum wage in Australia is $8.66, in France $8.88, in Italy $9.18, in England $9.20, and in Germany $12.74.)

Assuming fifty weeks at forty hours per week, this sets the U.S. minimum annual income at $10,300, below the poverty level, for tens of millions of Americans who have full-time jobs. The official poverty line in 2004 for a father or mother with one child was $12,490 in the continental United States, $14,360 in Hawaii, and $15,610 in Alaska. It is not surprising that our poorest people are suffering and that American citizens at all levels of income now have a lower percentage of equity in their homes than at any time in history.

Another gross example of subsidizing the wealthy involves my own lifetime profession of farming. Agricultural subsidies were a crucial factor in the survival of many farm families during the Great Depression, and were designed specifically for that purpose. These kinds of subsidies are still justified, but, perhaps not surprisingly, the rich farmers have harvested more federal government subsidies over the years, while poorer families have not been able to compete in Washington. During the last decade, we taxpayers have had to fork over an average of $14 billion annually for subsidies, of which 70 percent went to just 10 percent of the farmers, half to the top 3 percent, and one-fourth to the top 1 percent of recipients. The most fortunate American "farmer" received $7 million in

2002, and in Georgia, seven "farmers" received annual subsidies of more than $1 million! Thanks to powerful lobbyists, the worthy ideal of helping struggling farm families to survive has been abandoned. The U.S. Department of Agriculture estimated, in a report released in June 2005, that fewer than 25 percent of farms receive support payments.

Aside from this incredible disparity, U.S. subsidies wreak havoc in developing nations. A typical example is in Mali, where The Carter Center has a major project to help economic development. Three-fourths of Malians live on less than $1 a day, and 90 percent on less than $2. One quarter of its 12 million people depend directly on cotton for their livelihoods, and those families lucky enough to have the national average of five acres earn $280 a year. The chief obstacle to improving their lives is our country's cotton subsidies, which in some years drive down the world price to below the cost of Malian production. To put this into perspective, U.S. subsidy payments just to our cotton farmers are greater than the total national income of Mali, and double the amount of all American development assistance to sub-Saharan Africa. The World Trade Organization has ruled that our cotton subsidies are illegal, so this benevolent program, primarily for rich farmers, may have to be reformed.

These kinds of fundamental political and economic policies are not easy to explain or even to believe, and are a direct attack on American moral values, either in the political or the religious realm of life.

17

CONCLUSION:
WHAT IS A SUPERPOWER?

Americans have always been justifiably proud of our country, beginning with our forefathers' bold Declaration of Independence and their pronouncement "that all men are created equal, that they are endowed by their Creator with certain unalienable Rights, that among these are Life, Liberty and the pursuit of Happiness." Since then, our people have utilized America's great natural resources, access to warm oceans, relatively friendly neighbors, a heterogeneous population, and a pioneering spirit to form a "more perfect union."

Now, more than at any time in history, the United States of America has become the preeminent military power on earth. While there has been a sharp downward trend in worldwide expenditures for weapons during the past twenty years, the United States has continued to increase its military budget every year. It now exceeds $400 billion annually, equal to the total in all other nations combined. The next largest military budget is Russia's, which is one-sixth as large. The only arms race is one that we are having with ourselves. One reason for this enormous expenditure is that twenty thousand sailors and marines are deployed in ships afloat and almost three hundred thousand additional troops are stationed in more than 120 countries, with military bases in 63 of them. Since I left office, American presidents have intervened about fifty times in foreign countries. In addition to supplying our own military forces, America's arms manufacturers and those of our NATO allies provide 80 percent of weapon sales on the international market.

It is good to know that our nation's defenses against a conventional attack are impregnable, and imperative that America remain vigilant against threats from terrorists. But as is the case with a human being, admirable characteristics of a nation are not defined by size and physical prowess. What are some of the other attributes of a superpower? Once again, they might very well mirror those of a person. These would include a demonstrable commitment to truth, justice, peace, freedom, humility, human rights, generosity, and the upholding of other moral values.

There is no inherent reason that our nation cannot be the international example of these virtues. Our government should be known, without question, as opposed to war, dedicated to the resolution of disputes by peaceful means, and, whenever possible, eager to exert our tremendous capability and influence to accomplish this goal. We should be seen as the unswerving champion of freedom and human rights, both among our own citizens and within the global community. America should be the focal point around which other nations of all kinds could marshal to combat threats to security and to enhance the quality of our common environment. We should be in the forefront of providing humane assistance to people in need, willing to lead other industrialized nations in sharing some of our great wealth with those who are destitute.

In achieving all these goals, our great country should strive in every practical way to cooperate with other nations, most of which share these same fundamental ideals. There is an unprecedented opportunity as we enter this new millennium to use our unequaled influence wisely and with a generous spirit.

There would be no real sacrifice in exemplifying these traits. Instead, our own well-being would be enhanced by restoring the trust, admiration, and friendship that our nation formerly enjoyed among other peoples. At the same time, all Americans could be united at home in a common commitment to revive and nourish the religious faith and historic political and moral values that we have espoused and for which we have struggled during the past 230 years.

ACKNOWLEDGMENTS

My beliefs have been shaped by personal experiences as an evangelical Christian, a career officer in the U.S. Navy, and by a relatively brief career in public office.

I am grateful to my parents, teachers, and the religious, military, and political leaders who introduced me to the basic moral values exhibited in these three realms of American life. Above all, I am indebted to my wife, Rosalynn, who has been my greatest and most sustained blessing during our fifty-nine years together.

In preparing this text, I have derived great benefit from the intense discussions at Maranatha Baptist Church during weekly Sunday Bible lessons, where concepts of the Scriptures are melded with those of modern life. I want to express my thanks to members of our congregation and to the many visitors who come to share these experiences. In addition, our associates at The Carter Center have provided Rosalynn and me a continuing inter-relationship with many nations around the world, as we join forces to promote peace, alleviate suffering, and offer hope to some of the most destitute and abandoned people on earth.

Lauren Gay has been the link between me and the editors and publishers at Simon & Schuster, who have given me abundant help and advice in producing this book. Dr. Steve Hochman has been instrumental in checking the accuracy of the facts that are included, but the final responsibility for the text is mine.

ABOUT THE AUTHOR

JIMMY CARTER was born in Plains, Georgia, and served as thirty-ninth President of the United States. After this service, he and his wife, Rosalynn, founded The Carter Center, a nonprofit organization that prevents and resolves conflicts, enhances freedom and democracy, and improves health around the world. He is the author of numerous books, including *An Hour Before Daylight*, recognized as "an American classic." Since leaving the presidency in 1981, President Carter has earned a Nobel Peace Prize for his humanitarian work at The Carter Center.